The Navigator's Handbook

ESSENTIAL METHODS AND EQUIPMENT —

AND HOW TO USE THEM TO GO ANYWHERE AT SEA

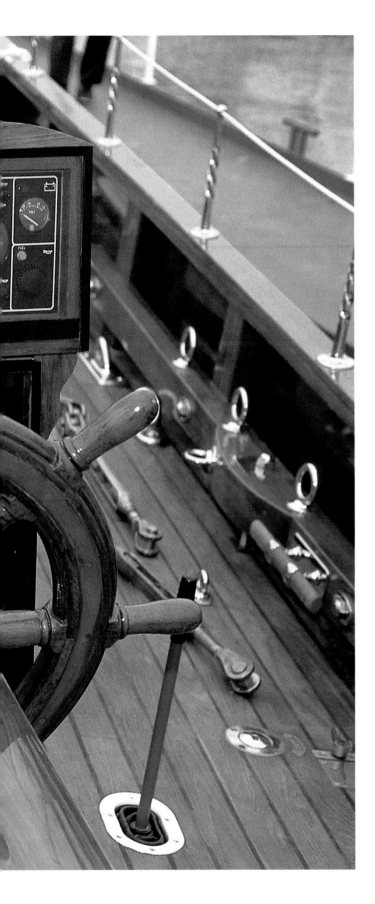

The Navigator's Handbook

ESSENTIAL METHODS AND EQUIPMENT —

AND HOW TO USE THEM TO GO ANYWHERE AT SEA

JEFF TOGHILL

THE LYONS PRESS

Guilford, Connecticut
An imprint of The Globe Pequot Press

Published in the United Kingdom, Republic of South Africa,
Australia and New Zealand by New Holland Publishers, Ltd.

First Lyons Press edition 2003

ISBN-13: 978-1-58574-791-7
ISBN-10: 1-58574-791-2

The Lyons Press is an imprint of The Globe Pequot Press

10 9 8 7 6 5 4 3 2

Reproduction by Hirt & Carter (Cape) (Pty) Ltd
Printed and bound in Malaysia

Library of Congress Cataloging-in-Publication Data is available on file

Author's acknowledgements

It would be impossible to mention everyone involved in such an extensive project as this. Most of the research work was done in the UK and Australia and I thank the many people on marinas and in boatyards who gave freely of their time and professional advice. Similarly, I am indebted to the many old and new sailing friends across the world, whose experiences in navigating small craft were invaluable. Raymarine (UK) and Oceantalk (Aus) kept me up to date on the latest in electronic equipment, as did the Litef company in Freiburg, Germany, with the latest laser gyro developments. Innumerable other firms provided much appreciated information.

On the personal side, my thanks to my nephew Stephen, for his assistance with the technical stuff, my sister-in-law, Elaine, for my UK 'office', and my publishers for their patience. As usual, my last but most important thanks go to my wife, Diana, who assisted throughout as secretary, researcher, photographer, general dogsbody and provider of moral support.

CONTENTS

INTRODUCTION

Since the dawn of time humans have found the need to practise navigation. The earliest Stone Age hunter, in paddling his coracle across a river, would have detected the set and drift of the current and countered it in order to reach his destination on the other side. Migrating Polynesians, using nothing more than a star reflected in a bowl of water, crossed vast stretches of the Pacific Ocean in their canoes. And adventurers like Marco Polo and Christopher Columbus opened up the world with primitive, but reasonably effective, forms of navigation.

And it is not just humans who have developed navigational skills. Every year millions of birds migrate across oceans and continents to avoid harsh winters and enjoy their favourite tropical climate. Eels and salmon return with unfailing accuracy to their breeding grounds, also thousands of miles across oceans. Indeed, it is difficult to visualize any aspect of life on this earth that does not somewhere invoke some form of navigation.

But nowhere are navigational skills more valuable and more practised than on the water. In harbours and estuaries, close to the coast or out on the open ocean, sailors in boats of all shapes and sizes need navigation to get them to their destination, then return them safely to their home port. Modern electronic navigation has made those journeys much safer and simpler, but the traditional skills are still widely practised and are still just as important, for the sea will quickly punish those who rely on good luck or good fortune.

This is particularly the case with boats and small craft. The sophisticated modern equipment and ideal conditions aboard large commercial vessels will readily cope with most navigational requirements. But navigators on yachts and small boats, using more basic equipment under more demanding conditions, need to be well prepared if they are to avoid the many problems that may be encountered once a passage has begun. Electronic navigation, despite its advantages, has limitations, particularly on small craft with sometimes vulnerable power sources. A sound knowledge of the basic traditional methods is essential if the voyage is to be a safe and successful one.

This book is designed to introduce the art of navigation to boat owners who are new to the subject, and will also provide a useful reference volume for those who want to keep abreast of developments in both traditional and modern methods of navigation.

In short, this book, together with membership of a club and good training, will ensure that the seafaring skills of navigators are never found wanting.

Opposite *Refinements to the older forms of navigation, and the development of sophisticated electronic systems, have made the handling and navigation of big ocean-going vessels a much simpler and more accurate exercise.*

Contents page *In 2001 Ellen MacArthur became the fastest woman to circumnavigate the globe.*

CHARTS AND PUBLICATIONS

NAUTICAL CHARTS

Nautical charts have been the basic tool for navigators for centuries of seafaring. In essence, they are similar to the motorist's road map, as both are used as a means of getting from one point to another. However, where a road map provides necessary information to navigate across the land and ignores the seaward side of the coast, the nautical chart deals mostly with the sea and carries land information of use to the mariner. While a road map provides details of towns, villages and roads, a nautical chart is concerned with water depths, reefs, shoals and other features of use in navigating offshore.

Most charts are produced by what's known as a 'Hydrographic Office' (usually part of the local naval organization) and these are known as Admiralty or Naval charts. However, there are some fine charts produced by private publishers and these can be of use in coastal areas or harbours that are not covered in sufficient detail by the official charts. Boat chandlers (suppliers of shipping or yachting equipment) carry a range of both types and before setting out on a passage a wise navigator will spend some time at the chandlers selecting the best charts to suit his or her purposes.

THE SCALE OF A CHART

Charts cover virtually the entire world, so there are charts of different scales to provide the necessary detail for different areas. An ocean chart, for example, which covers a large area

Opposite *Fathom charts have the depths (soundings) in fathoms, while metric charts have soundings in metres. Eventually, all charts will be metric.*

of the world, could not provide fine detail of each bay or harbour along the coastlines it covers, so charts of larger scales are required to meet the needs of differing navigational requirements.

Charts come in three main scales:

- Small-scale charts, which cover large stretches of coastline;
- Medium-scale charts, which cover coastal regions in moderate detail;
- Large-scale charts, which provide the fine detail of harbours and close inshore waters.

MERCATOR'S PROJECTION

In order to find their way around the earth, navigators have divided the surface of the globe into a grid: the vertical scale is latitude (expressed as horizontal lines), extending from 0° at the equator to 90° at the poles; the horizontal scale is longitude (expressed as vertical lines), which commences at 0° at the Greenwich Meridian and extends east and west around the globe for 180° to the Midnight Meridian. Between them, these two scales provide co-ordinates for locating positions anywhere on earth's surface.

One of the problems with sea navigation is that it must be done on a flat chart, yet the earth is round. How to flatten out the round surface of the globe onto a chart without distortion was a mesmerizing puzzle that exercised the minds of mathematicians and navigators for centuries, until a Dutchman named Mercator came up with a simple, albeit not foolproof, solution. Mercator's Projection, introduced in 1569 and used to this day, is best explained this way:

Imagine the world as a plastic globe with a light inside it; this globe is placed inside a paper cylinder. When the light is switched on, the lines of latitude and longitude on the curved surface of the globe are projected outward onto the inner surface of the cylinder as straight lines. These lines are traced onto the cylinder.

When the cylinder is unrolled, a flat representation of the grid appears, with the lines of latitude and longitude running horizontally and vertically across it. To reduce this distortion, the segment near the centre of the projection is used.

Today mathematical formulae are used to achieve the same end, and these reduce any distortion to a negligible amount.

Right *Mercator's Projection involves converting the curved surface of the earth into the flat surface of a chart. Only the very centre of the projection is used in order to minimize the distortion.*

The world globe is divided into a grid of latitude and longitude; this grid matches those carried on the chart.

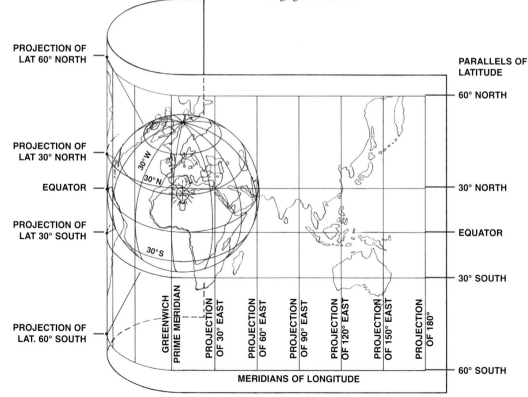

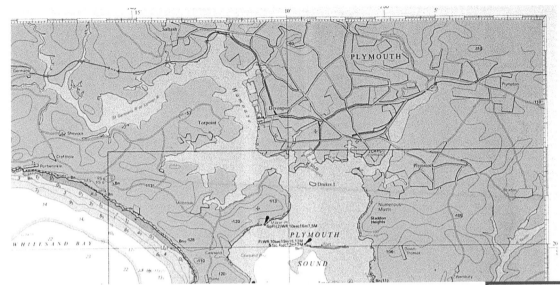

THE LATITUDE AND LONGITUDE GRID

The latitude and longitude grid is shown on the chart with the lines of latitude running across the chart, parallel to the equator (they are termed Parallels of Latitude), and with the latitude scale on either side of the chart.

Positions are always give with latitude first, then longitude – the opposite convention holds for ordinance survey maps.

The Meridian of Longitude lines run vertically up and down the chart, with the longitude scale carried across the top and bottom.

Unlike latitude, the meridians of longitude are not parallel. Since they run from pole to pole, dividing the globe into 360°, they converge at the poles, rather like the segments of an orange.

Using latitude and longitude co-ordinates

There are a number of ways in which the latitude and longitude scales can be used to plot a boat's position on the chart or, alternatively, to find the latitude and longitude of a position already on the chart.

The traditional method uses parallel rules and dividers, although some navigators prefer to use protractors and other patented instruments – most of which are just as accurate.

To plot a position from latitude and longitude co-ordinates, the parallel rules are first laid along a nearby parallel of latitude and then slid carefully upward or downward until the edge of the rules touches the latitude required on the scale at the side of the chart.

A pencil line drawn along this edge of the rule will lay off the latitude across the chart ('lay off' is the nautical term for drawing a line across a chart).

The dividers are then placed with one point on the nearest meridian of longitude and the other on the actual longitude required, using the top or bottom scale. The navigator next transfers the dividers to the newly drawn latitude line, and the longitude is measured along this line to provide the position required.

To determine the latitude and longitude co-ordinates of a position that is known, the navigator simply reverses the procedure: the parallel rules are placed to run through the known position and the latitude is read off on the side scale. Dividers are used to measure the longitude from the nearest meridian.

Above *By measuring nautical miles from the latitude scale on either side of the chart with dividers, distances can be stepped off across the chart.*

THE NAUTICAL MILE

Because the world is a sphere of 360°, all measurements on it are made in degrees (°) and minutes (there are 60 minutes in a degree), including the measurement of distance.

As mentioned, the meridians of longitude converge toward the poles and, except at the equator, are not consistently spaced. Longitude, therefore, is not suitable as a distance measurement, which is why the consistently spaced parallels of latitude are used: one minute of latitude = one nautical mile.

All distance measurements are read in minutes from the latitude scales on either side of the chart. Although scales in statute miles (land miles) and metres are also usually carried somewhere on the chart, they are never used for navigational workings.

For comparison with linear measurement: one nautical mile = 6080 feet or 1853 metres.

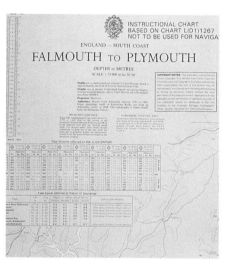

Above *The chart title contains much useful information about navigational hazards in the area it covers.*

Right top *A traditional (cardinal) compass card.*

Right bottom *The compass rose is printed at strategic points across the chart.*

THE CHART TITLE

The title is located at some convenient point on the chart and carries a great deal of information relevant to its use, including:

- the area covered
- the scale of the chart
- whether the soundings are in feet or metres
- the projection
- datums for height of objects and depths
- information on tides
- other useful navigational data.

THE COMPASS ROSE

A compass rose is a replica of a 360° compass card. A number of compass roses are printed at convenient points across the chart to facilitate the easy transfer of compass readings to and from the chart.

In this way a course laid down on the chart can be read off the compass rose and transferred to the master compass for the helmsman to steer.

A compass bearing of a shore object can likewise be transferred to the chart by means of the compass rose and can be used to plot the position of the boat.

The compass rose lies in the north/south plane of longitude and indicates the direction of the geographic north pole, so its readings are said to be 'true'. Unfortunately magnetic compasses relate to earth's magnetic pole, which is not in the same place as the geographic pole. Because of this, readings on the compass need adjustment before they can be used on the chart, and chart readings need adjustment before they can be used with the compass.

'Variation' is the term given to the difference between true and magnetic readings and can be described as the error in the compass caused by earth's magnetism. This varies across the world, but is listed in the centre of the compass rose for each area. The application of magnetic compass errors is described in detail on pages 24–26.

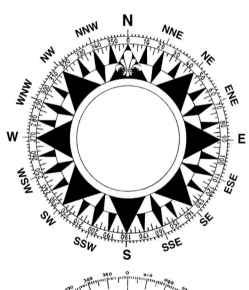

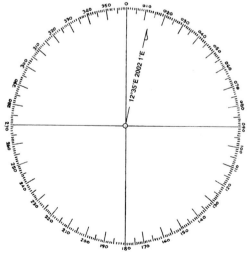

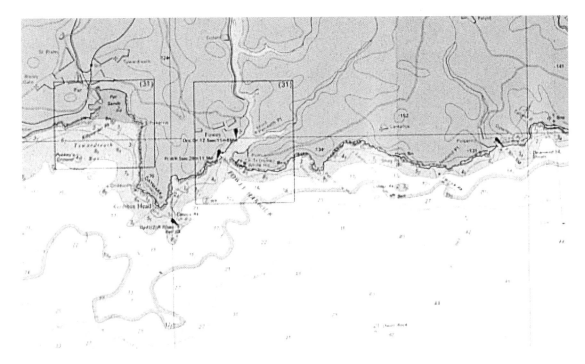

SOUNDINGS

The depth of water is obviously of prime importance in boat navigation, and the whole of the sea area of a chart is covered with small figures indicating depths. These figures are known as 'soundings' and represent the depth of water below a reference level known as 'chart datum'.

On UK charts, this is the level of the lowest tide that can be predicted (lowest astronomical tide), and so there will rarely be less water over the sea bed than that indicated on the chart. Charts produced by other authorities do not necessarily use the same datum, so it is important to check the datum used.

It must be taken into consideration, when using the soundings for navigation, that the sounder reading must be adjusted for the height of the tide at the time. This is dealt with in more detail on page 69.

HEIGHTS

The heights of shore objects that are readily visible from seaward, such as prominent buildings, mountains or lighthouses, are marked on the chart.

Such objects can be useful in close coastal navigation, and their height above sea level is required for the plotting calculations. The heights of bridges and overhead cables are also given, and these heights are measured above the average highest high water in the tidal cycle. This is again a safety factor, as there will then rarely, if ever, be less clearance under a bridge or cables than that marked on the chart.

CONTOURS

The contours of hills are indicated on a chart, just as they are on a land map, by lines joining equal elevations. Contours of the sea bed are indicated in much the same way, by using lines joining equal depths. The depth or height represented by the contour is indicated by a small figure inside it.

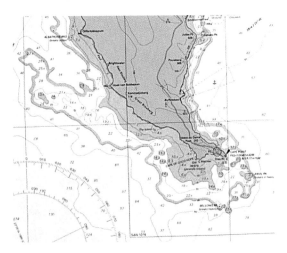

LIGHTS AND LIGHTHOUSES

Lighthouses, sometimes called the 'mariner's sign-posts', are carefully positioned at strategic points along the coast and at the entrance to harbours.

Buoys and **beacons** are used to provide daytime and nighttime assistance to navigators in estuaries and rivers. During daylight, they can be identified by their colours (clearly marked on the chart), and at night by their colour and flash characteristics. These characteristics are given in an abbreviated form, described on page 48. Other abbreviations indicate the height and range of each light.

Ocean lights are established in major lighthouses along the coastline and shine out over the open sea to provide guidance for vessels well offshore, particularly those making a landfall. These lights may have a range of up to 25 or 30 nautical miles and are usually white.

Coastal lights are used to provide guidance for coastal navigators. They are located at regular intervals along a coastline and have a medium range (8–15 nautical miles), which ensures that on most coastlines there is always at least one in sight, thus providing continuity for night navigation. These lights may be white or coloured and may be strategically placed to guide vessels into a harbour.

Harbour lights, as their name denotes, are short-range lights (1–10 nautical miles) located in a harbour or estuary to guide vessels past shoals, along channels or to indicate dangers. They may be fitted to beacons or buoys and use a number of different colours, most often red, green or white.

Left Long-range ocean and coastal lights usually have high-powered rotating beams created by fresnel lenses.

Inset Harbour lights can be located on piles or beacons, or on floating buoys.

Right An excerpt from a publication listing the symbols and abbreviations used on charts.

PUBLICATIONS

In addition to charts, a number of publications are available to mariners to help make navigation safer and more accurate. The principal publications, which can be obtained from any good boat chandler, are indicated on the following pages.

SYMBOLS AND ABBREVIATIONS

Because a chart is used for navigational workings, it is important that it is not cluttered with too much information, especially in the seaward areas where plotting takes place. By the same token it is equally important that all the information a navigator requires for safe navigation is provided in full detail.

To achieve both these requirements, symbols and abbreviations are used to mark important features on the chart, and the key to these is published in a separate chart or handbook. US Chart 1 and British Admiralty Publication 5011 contain the explanations for all symbols and abbreviations used on the internationally used US and British charts.

NOTICES TO MARINERS

Like any map, a chart can quickly become outdated. Light characteristics may be changed, buoyage systems altered or channels moved, which all render a chart inaccurate. Unless the chart is updated, such changes can create serious problems for the navigator and even compromise the safety of the vessel.

Official charts published by the maritime authority of any country are updated periodically by means of 'Notices to Mariners'.

These are a kind of mariners' newspaper, issued frequently, which indicate in detail anything that may affect safe navigation. The notices contain information on many different aspects of navigation, but in particular with changes to charts.

When a change needs to be made to something on a chart, it is made in pencil if the change is temporary, and in purple ink when permanent.

The date and number of the Notice to Mariners used to make the correction is recorded at the bottom left of the chart so a navigator can tell at a glance if the chart is up to date.

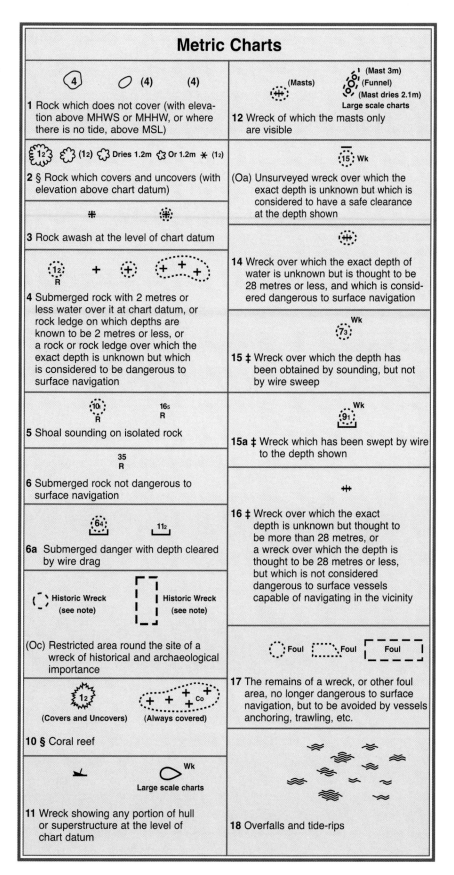

Metric Charts

1 Rock which does not cover (with elevation above MHWS or MHHW, or where there is no tide, above MSL)

2 § Rock which covers and uncovers (with elevation above chart datum)

3 Rock awash at the level of chart datum

4 Submerged rock with 2 metres or less water over it at chart datum, or rock ledge on which depths are known to be 2 metres or less, or a rock or rock ledge over which the exact depth is unknown but which is considered to be dangerous to surface navigation

5 Shoal sounding on isolated rock

6 Submerged rock not dangerous to surface navigation

6a Submerged danger with depth cleared by wire drag

Historic Wreck (see note)   Historic Wreck (see note)

(Oc) Restricted area round the site of a wreck of historical and archaeological importance

10 § Coral reef   (Covers and Uncovers)   (Always covered)

11 Wreck showing any portion of hull or superstructure at the level of chart datum   Wk Large scale charts

12 Wreck of which the masts only are visible   (Masts)   (Mast 3m) (Funnel) (Mast dries 2.1m) Large scale charts

(Oa) Unsurveyed wreck over which the exact depth is unknown but which is considered to have a safe clearance at the depth shown   15 Wk

14 Wreck over which the exact depth of water is unknown but is thought to be 28 metres or less, and which is considered dangerous to surface navigation

15 ‡ Wreck over which the depth has been obtained by sounding, but not by wire sweep   Wk 73

15a ‡ Wreck which has been swept by wire to the depth shown   Wk 91

16 ‡ Wreck over which the exact depth is unknown but thought to be more than 28 metres, or a wreck over which the depth is thought to be 28 metres or less, but which is not considered dangerous to surface vessels capable of navigating in the vicinity

17 The remains of a wreck, or other foul area, no longer dangerous to surface navigation, but to be avoided by vessels anchoring, trawling, etc.   Foul   Foul   Foul

18 Overfalls and tide-rips

SAILING DIRECTIONS

Sometime called 'Pilots', these are the navigator's 'guide books' and act as a supplement to the chart. They contain detailed information on all navigational features related to a section of coastline and adjacent waters that could not be carried on the chart. Particularly they refer to local phenomena such as tidal anomalies, local coast currents, military exercises, changes to harbour buoyage, etc.

Sailing Directions are updated from the Notices to Mariners so that they are current and accurate.

There are a number of types of pilot available. The most extensive are those produced by the Hydrographic Office, which cover the entire world in a series of hardcover books; at the other end of the scale are the local pilots, often produced by private publishers or local maritime authorities, even perhaps by local yacht clubs.

Providing they are accurate and kept up to date by corrections from Notices to Mariners, these Sailing Directions provide vital information essential to safe navigation.

TIDE TABLES

Of prime importance when working close inshore, and particularly in harbours or estuaries, tide tables provide predictions of tidal movements for a full year. Such predictions include times and heights of high and low water, and in some cases indications of tidal flow. Once again, these volumes may be produced by official sources or private publishers, and are available from boat chandlers.

Most tide tables provide predictions in two sections: daily information on tides for standard ports; and adjustments for time and height for secondary ports, based on a designated standard port.

They are fairly self-explanatory and all readings of depths are related to chart datum as a safety measure. Tide heights taken from the tide tables are added to the soundings on the chart, ensuring that rarely will there be less water than that indicated on the chart.

LIGHT LISTS

This is a volume carrying details of every navigation light on a specified coastline. Information on the height, range, characteristic and colour of the light are given, as well as its geographical position and any other useful details. These lists are also updated by means of Notices to Mariners. (Some hydrographic offices offer publications in CD format.)

OTHER PUBLICATIONS

There are, of course, many other publications that can be of use to boat navigators. Reference books on instruments, particularly electronic instruments, need to be kept on board, and almanacs and tables for use with celestial navigation are necessary if the boat is going deep sea. The main requirements for these are described from page 82 for celestial navigation and page 86 for electronic navigation.

CHART INSTRUMENTS

Nautical charts are usually printed on durable paper, which means that the navigator's workings for one

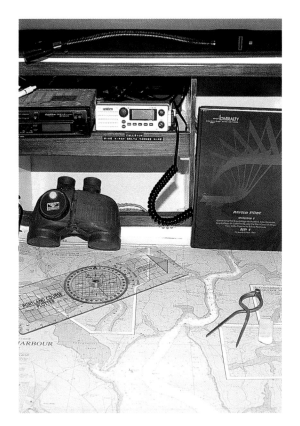

Above A major offshore light-house comes in for a battering.

journey can be erased easily and the chart used over and over. Some boat owners like to cover the surface of the chart with a plastic overlay or have it laminated, in order to reduce wear and tear.

As a general rule, though, working directly onto the paper surface does not do much damage to the chart, as long as the plotting and course laying is always done with a soft pencil such as a 2B.

A set of parallel rules, preferably the roller type, also reduces the wear and tear on the chart. The traditional sliding rules are fine, but aboard small craft, where things may get a little damp, sliding rules tend to stick on spots of water on the chart. Some navigators prefer protractors for their chart work, and there are a number of patented devices that can be used with great accuracy.

Measurements of distance are made by using a pair of marine (single handed) dividers (when using dividers, it is important not to stick the points into the paper too firmly or it will wind up with pock marks all over the surface). A pair of compasses can also come in handy when drawing circles of danger or position.

Traditionally these instruments have provided navigators with all the tools they need to lay off courses and plot positions on a chart, and it is difficult to imagine that they will not remain popular for many years. Nevertheless, there are numerous other instruments to be found in chandlery stores, all intended to make plotting quicker and easier.

Left A wide range of instruments can be used for chart work. Among the most useful are single-handed dividers and a Portland plotter or protractor.

Instruments and
Aids to Navigation

Modern electronics provide a wide range of instruments for use in navigation, but traditional instruments still have their place, especially in small craft, and the basic requirements are rather simple.

THE MAGNETIC COMPASS

The focal point of all navigation on vessels both large and small is the compass. It has assisted navigators in their voyages across the oceans for untold centuries, and although modern electronic compasses have been developed in recent decades, the traditional compass, which uses earth's magnetism, is little changed from the original and is still widely used. It is particularly well suited to small craft, as it requires no electrical or mechanical power source. Indeed, it is so efficient and reliable that it is still carried in ocean-going ships as a back-up for their sophisticated electronic equipment.

In one form or another, the magnetic compass is familiar to almost everyone. The simplest type is the boy scout's compass, where a magnetized needle, freely suspended over a compass card, aligns itself with the earth's magnetic north/south line. In more sophisticated compasses, magnetic needles are attached beneath a freely suspended compass card so that as the needles swing into the north/south line they turn the card with them. This makes it easier to read the card, and when the whole unit is placed in a bowl of fluid (usually a water and alcohol mix), the compass stabilizes and is 'damped' (slowed down) to reduce the swinging effect in a

Opposite *A well-equipped boat will carry traditional and electronic navigation instruments. Here a compass sits among a range of electronic equipment.*

Right top *A typical readout for a digital compass. These avoid the swing of a magnetic compass card.*

Right bottom *The construction of a typical marine card compass.*

Below *The steering compass is usually housed in a binnacle in front of the helmsman. Correcting magnets may be placed around it to counter the effect of any magnetism in the boat, particularly in steel-hulled vessels.*

seaway, making it even easier to read. This is the basic form of magnetic compass used in small craft.

Traditionally, the card was graduated in the cardinal points of the compass (N, S, E, W), and there are still a number of manufacturers that prefer this type of marking. But for ease of use, most compasses have replaced the cardinal points with three-figure notation, in which the edge of the card is graduated from 0° to 360°.

A line on the rim of the compass bowl (the container in which the compass is mounted), known as the 'lubber line', indicates the direction in which the boat is heading. By swinging (turning) the boat until the required course – in three-figure notation – lies against the lubber line, the helmsman aligns the boat's head with the direction to be steered.

THE STEERING COMPASS

Most yachts and small sailing craft carry two compasses on board: one to steer by and one to use for obtaining bearings.

The master, or steering, compass is located in a position where it can be easily seen by the helmsman – usually at the steering position. Like all magnetic compasses, it can be affected by outside magnetic influences, such as metal, other magnets and electrical circuits. These must all be taken into account when installing the steering compass in order to reduce to a minimum the risk of any errors being introduced into the compass.

As a general rule, all metal objects, or anything that may affect the compass, must be kept at least one metre away. (Electrical equipment often specifies a 'compass safe distance'.) Electric wiring, especially circuits or coils, must also be kept outside the radius. When the boat is checked for magnetic error (see page 23), it may be necessary to screen or move any objects or circuits that interfere with the compass.

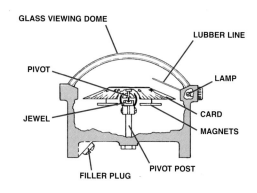

The hand-bearing compass is subject to the same magnetic errors as the steering compass, but these can vary when the compass is moved to different locations around the boat. For this reason it is important to check for any changes before taking bearings. This is done by aligning the hand-bearing compass with the boat's head at the point where the compass is to be used, and checking it against the heading (course) on the steering compass (see page 22).

Experienced navigators usually take all bearings from a predetermined position on the boat, where shore objects are clearly visible and the hand-bearing compass has been previously checked.

THE HAND-BEARING COMPASS

This is a portable compass used for taking bearings for navigational calculations and plots. The steering compass is often located in a position where taking bearings is difficult, such as in a heeled (leaning) yacht where it is not possible to sight the compass over the high side.

The advantage of the hand-bearing compass is that it can be carried by hand around the boat to points more suited to taking bearings.

It is usually smaller than the master or steering compass, and is fitted with some form of sighting device so that the object being used for bearings can be aligned in the sight and the compass bearing read off the compass card. (Rather like a rifle sight, the object is 'aligned' by being centred in the sight – usually a 'v' or fine line. Hand-bearing compasses are always fitted with a sight.)

There are many different types of hand-bearing compasses on the market and it is important to try each type in order to find the most accurate and the easiest to use.

Left top To reduce the swing of the card and make steering easier, most yacht compasses consist of a dome or globe filled with a fluid that 'dampens' any severe movement. It also allows the compass card to remain level when the yacht heels.

Left In traditional vessels, the visual effect of brass binnacles and cardinal compass cards enhances the appearance of the timber deck fittings.

Left The hand-bearing compass can be carried around the deck until a suitable place for sighting shore objects is found. It is then lined up with the required object and a bearing is read off.

EARTH'S MAGNETIC FIELD

The earth is, in effect, a huge magnet surrounded by a magnetic field. This field radiates from the poles and can be best understood by studying the old school physics experiment where a sheet of paper is laid over a magnet and then sprinkled with iron filings. The iron filings align themselves with the paths of the magnetic 'lines of force' running from the poles around the outside of the magnet, revealing a pattern known as a 'magnetic field'.

When a magnetized needle is introduced into this field, it also aligns itself with the lines of force.

The earth's magnetic field is similar in shape, with the lines of force running from the poles, around the earth. When a magnetic compass is placed in this field it aligns itself with the lines of force, the north end of the compass card pointing toward the magnetic north pole. Since the card is free to swing, it will remain in this attitude no matter how the boat moves around.

COMPASS ERROR

All magnetic compasses are subject to errors caused by outside magnetic influences, mostly from the earth's magnetic field or from magnetism in the boat. These latter errors can be determined, reduced or eliminated; others can be tabulated and applied to compass readings so that accurate results can be obtained for steering or navigation work.

The two principal errors are called 'deviation' and 'variation': deviation is the error in the compass caused by the boat's magnetism; variation is the error in the compass caused by the fact that the magnetic poles do not correspond with the geographic poles.

DEVIATION

As described earlier, magnetic influences that can create errors in the compass readings are present in every vessel. Some have relatively little effect, but some can considerably affect the compass.

Imagine, for example, the effect of placing a compass on board a steel-hulled yacht; the magnetism in the steel would seriously affect the reading of the compass card. Similarly, placing the compass in the cockpit immediately above the engine can send the compass card spinning when alternators, generators and other electrical equipment come into use. The error induced into the compass by such factors is known as 'deviation'.

Fortunately deviation can be reduced and sometimes eliminated by compensating the compass with counter-magnets. In fibreglass boats, for instance, there will probably be only a few metal fittings near the compass, and with a little forethought when the boat is fitted out, electrical wiring can be strategically placed so that overall there will be only slight deviation, which can be easily removed.

By contrast, the steel-hulled yacht with its major deviation problem will need considerable compensation to reduce the deviation to a manageable level. A compass adjuster is a person skilled in this work and a new boat, or one that has been recently refitted, should be turned over to such a person who will take it out from the shore, determine the amount of deviation, then set about reducing or eliminating it.

Right *This illustrates the magnetic field of force that flows from one pole to another around a magnet. A magnetized needle placed anywhere in this field will align itself with the flow – i.e. it will point to one of the poles.*

Right *Earth's magnetic field of force follows the same trend, and a compass needle in this field will point toward the north pole. Because the magnetic and true poles are not in the same position, a magnetic compass does not point toward true north, as do electronic compasses such as the gyro. The difference between 'true' and 'magnetic' readings is called 'variation'.*

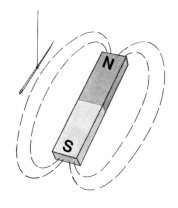

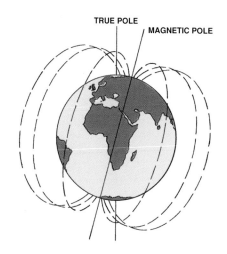

TRUE POLE   MAGNETIC POLE

DEVIATION CARD

Vessel: *Marie Louise*

Boat's head		Deviation
N	000	*0*
NE	045	*2E*
E	090	*4E*
SE	135	*2E*
S	180	*0*
SW	225	*2W*
W	270	*4W*
NW	315	*2W*
N	360	*0*

Swinging the compass

Deviation is constant as long as the boat remains on one heading (on one course), so it is obviously important to establish the exact amount of deviation for each heading.

If a compass adjuster is not available, the navigator will need to handle this him- or herself. The procedure is known as 'swinging the compass' and should be carried out before the boat sets out on any extended voyage, particularly if any structural or fitting changes have taken place.

The boat is taken into clear water and then anchored or moored so that she lies on a north heading. Two nearby shore objects must be aligned in transit (in line with one another) with their true bearing read from the chart, and then a magnetic bearing of the same transit taken on the compass. The true bearing taken from the chart and the bearing of the transits read on the compass will be different – this difference is called Compass Error, a combination of Variation and Deviation. However, only the deviation is required, as variation is listed in the compass rose of every chart.

To find deviation, variation must be removed from the compass error just established. This is done as described on page 26 and the resulting deviation is then listed on a deviation card against the boat's heading (north).

Since deviation changes as the boat's head changes, the procedure is carried out again, this time with the boat set on each of the remaining cardinal headings: E, S and W. Then a repeat performance, taking readings on the inter-cardinal headings of NE, SE, SW and NW, completes the operation. The deviation on each heading is then tabulated and a 'deviation card' made up for future reference. Deviation from this table is applied to all compass readings according to the direction of the boat's head.

Compensating the compass with counter magnets to eliminate deviation should not be attempted by amateurs, as incorrect placement of the magnets could upset the compass and induce other errors.

Left *A typical small boat deviation card.*

Below *Apart from using them for swinging the compass, transit bearings are useful when manoeuvring in narrow waterways, anchoring and in other navigational work. Any two objects in line create a transit, but ideally the front object should be lower than the rear, and both should be well spaced to indicate immediately any change of bearing.*

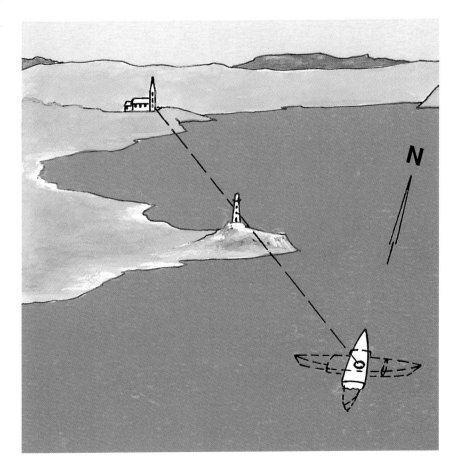

VARIATION

Variation is constant for any heading, but does change as the vessel moves across the ocean. It is the result of earth's magnetic poles being out of alignment with the geographic poles. The amount (in degrees and minutes) that magnetic north is out of alignment with true north is the amount of deflection of the compass caused by variation.

Unlike deviation, variation cannot be compensated for or removed but must be allowed whenever a compass is used. The amount of variation required to correct a compass reading at any given spot is indicated on the chart in the centre of each compass rose. Variation changes slightly from year to year, and the amount of change is also noted in the compass rose. Charts showing the lines of variation are available at chart agents and boat chandlers.

Right *Variation is consistent at any given spot on the earth's surface and is indicated in the compass rose on the relevant chart. Variation charts covering large areas of the world are available, if required.*

Below *If the compass error is not taken into consideration, the boat will not follow the course it is steering.*

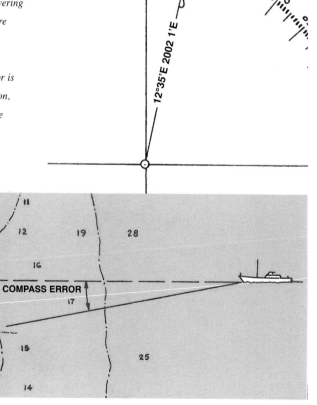

APPLYING COMPASS ERROR

Once the amount of deviation and variation affecting the compass has been determined, it must be applied to convert all compass readings to true readings for use on the chart. It may also be used to convert true readings taken from the chart to magnetic readings, so they can be applied to the compass. Deviation and variation are named East or West and if both are present, they are usually combined by adding like names or subtracting unlike names:

Variation	12°E
Deviation	6°W
Total compass error	6°E

They are then applied as follows: 'Error east, compass least. Error west, compass best.'

This useful little jingle, used by amateur and professional navigators alike, indicates that if the combined compass error is named East, it must be applied so that the compass reading is least or less than the true reading. Similarly, if the error is named West, the compass reading must be best or better than the true reading.

An example, using the above error names, will make it clearer:

Course to steer as laid on the chart	014° True
Compass error	6°E
(Error east, compass least)	
Compass course to steer	008° Compass
Bearing from hand-bearing (HB) compass	245°C
Compass error	6°E
(Error east, compass least)	
True bearing to lay off on the chart	251°T

Similarly, if the error is west:

Course to steer from chart	014°T
Error	6°W
(Error west, compass best)	
Compass course to steer	020°C
Bearing from HB compass	245°C
Error	6°W
(Error west, compass best)	
Bearing to lay off on chart	239°T

OTHER COMPASSES

Although the magnetic compass is still universally used in small craft, some modern compasses are beginning to appear as electronics make inroads into traditional navigation methods.

The gyro compass is an accurate, electrically driven compass. It does not suffer from variation or deviation errors and has been used in ships for many decades. (The first gyroscope was invented in 1852, and gyro compasses have been used in naval ships since the early 20th century.) While a gyro compass is sometimes carried in a large yacht, generally speaking they are too expensive and subject to errors from the extreme motion of small vessels, and are thus not suitable for the average family yacht.

Ring laser gyro compasses (see Electronic Navigation, page 114) are at the leading edge of navigation technology, but are even more impractical for small vessels; they are large and very expensive – they can cost at least eight to ten times as much as a standard gyro. The standard gyro is based on a spinning wheel, while the ring laser gyro uses a ring of light.

A recent development using fibreoptics to carry the laser beam is being produced in a form that is better suited (in both size and cost) to small craft.

Known as FOG (Fibreoptic Gyro), this seems to be the most promising version of an electronic compass for yachts to date. Like the standard gyro compass, it is not affected by either variation or deviation.

Fluxgate sensor compasses have become popular in recent times and are well suited to leisure craft. These compasses convert internal magnetic compass readings into digital data, which are corrected mathematically rather than physically, so that the readout is automatically corrected for any deviation in the boat.

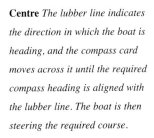

Left *Many different versions of the magnetic compass are available. This is a yacht racing compass.*

Centre *The lubber line indicates the direction in which the boat is heading, and the compass card moves across it until the required compass heading is aligned with the lubber line. The boat is then steering the required course.*

Left *Electronic compasses such as the gyro, fibreoptic gyro and fluxgate mostly provide digital readouts. However, many people prefer a compass card to read-out, as it is easier to see the rate of turn.*

THE SEXTANT

Although it is often used for coastal navigation, the sextant is more frequently used for celestial sight taking. Indeed, it is the mainstay of celestial navigation and is used in conjunction with a chronometer (a very accurate clock).

The sextant measures the angle of a heavenly body above the horizon. This is done by reflecting an image of the body – the sun, star, planet or moon – through two mirrors, one of which is fixed and one moveable.

The horizon is observed through one side of the fixed mirror, which has clear glass, and the sextant arm, which carries the moveable mirror, is adjusted until a reflection of the heavenly body is brought down and positioned on this horizon. The number of degrees and minutes of arc that the body is lowered is recorded on the sextant arc. This is the angle of the body above the horizon and is known as its 'altitude'.

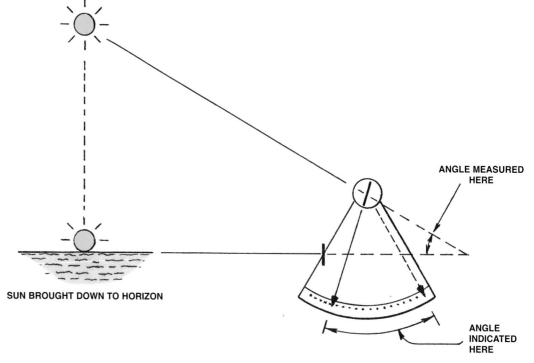

SUN BROUGHT DOWN TO HORIZON

ANGLE MEASURED HERE

ANGLE INDICATED HERE

PARTS OF A SEXTANT

- Telescope: used to magnify the heavenly body for greater accuracy in sight taking.
- Index mirror: The upper mirror, which is mounted on and moves with the index arm.
- Index arm: The moving part of the sextant, which adjusts the angle of the index mirror, and records the amount of movement on a graduated arc.
- Arc: The scale along the bottom of the sextant, which measures the angle of the heavenly body in degrees when a sight is taken.
- Shades: Coloured glass shades situated in front of both mirrors to reduce the glare of the sun.
- Micrometer screw: a Vernier scale drum, which allows fine adjustment of the reading to be made in minutes or seconds of arc.

- Horizon mirror: The fixed mirror on the frame of the instrument, which is half-silvered so that the heavenly body is reflected on one side and the horizon sighted through the clear glass on the other.

ERRORS OF THE SEXTANT

Like the magnetic compass, the sextant is subject to errors that must be eliminated or allowed for in the sight reading.

The errors concern the setting of the mirrors, for in order to take accurate sights both mirrors must be precisely parallel to each other and precisely perpendicular to the plane of the instrument. Before any sights are taken, the sextant must be checked and any errors removed; this is part of the daily routine when sight taking on a long ocean passage.

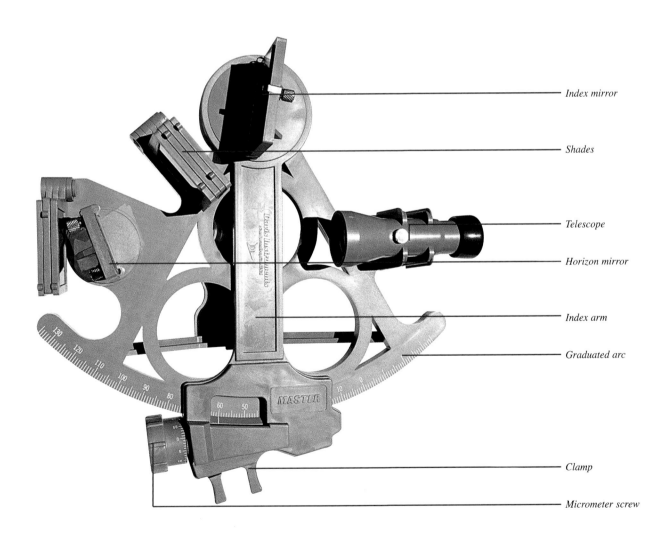

Index mirror

Shades

Telescope

Horizon mirror

Index arm

Graduated arc

Clamp

Micrometer screw

Above *When the sextant is set at zero, the true and reflected horizons should form an unbroken line. If not, index error is present.*

Below *If the horizon separates when the sextant is tilted to one side, then side error is present.*

Index error

This occurs when the two mirror faces are not parallel. Check for index error and remove it as follows:

1. Set the index arc at zero (0°) on the scale and micrometer screw.
2. Point the sextant at the horizon and look through the telescope. If both true and reflected horizons create one straight line, there is no error.
3. If the horizon is broken, adjust the index arm until both images create a straight line. The amount of error can then be read off the micrometer screw.

4. The error can be removed by adjusting the small screw on the back of the horizon mirror, closest to the body of the instrument until the horizon forms one straight line.

Side error

This is the result of the horizon mirror not being exactly perpendicular to the plane of the sextant. The following routine is used to check and remove side error:

1. Set the index arc at zero (0°) and point the sextant at the horizon. If index error has already been corrected, the horizon should appear in one straight line.
2. Tilt the sextant to one side for at least 45°.
3. If the true and reflected horizons do not stay in a straight line, side error is present. This cannot be read off; the error must be removed.
4. Turn the small screw on the back of the horizon mirror farthest from the instrument until the horizons form one straight line.

Perpendicularity

This is the error that occurs when the index mirror is not perpendicular to the plane of the sextant body. Determining and removing this error is a little more difficult than the previous two, and may need some practice. The procedure is as follows:

1. Set the index arm roughly in the middle of the arc.
2. Turn the sextant around so that the observer looks from the top of the instrument into the index mirror. A reflection of the index arc will be seen and this should be in alignment with the true index arc seen by looking past the index mirror.
3. If the true and reflected arcs are not in alignment an error exists and must be removed by adjusting the small screw on the back of the index mirror.

Adjusting for an error in one mirror can create an error in another, so it is important that all three errors are corrected together, adjusting the mirrors one after the other until all errors have been removed. The only error which can be tolerated is index error, and then only if the amount is less than 5 minutes of arc. In this case it can be read off, as described, and allowed as an

adjustment to the sight. Otherwise the error should be removed by adjusting the inside screw on the back of the horizon mirror.

Checking for errors at night

The procedure for perpendicularity is the same as for daylight hours, but for the other errors a star is used instead of the horizon.

Many navigators prefer to check the sextant at night, as the small size of a star makes for more accurate adjustment. Others find that holding the sextant pointing toward the sky for any length of time can be tiring. Either system can be used, providing the checks are made each time the sextant is used.

A slight bump, a change of temperature or accidentally handling the mirrors when taking the sextant out of its case are just a few of the actions that can induce errors into this sensitive instrument, hence the need to check it before each use.

While initially the procedure may seem laborious, it becomes simple routine after a while.

Left *Index and side error can be checked using the sun. When the sextant is set at zero, true and reflected suns should appear as one. If they separate horizontally, side error is present; if they separate vertically, index error is present. The same method can be used at night with a star.*

Left centre *When sighted at an oblique angle into the index mirror, true and reflected arcs should be in alignment – at the point indicated by the arrow. If these are not in alignment, there is an error of perpendicularity.*

TAKING SEXTANT SIGHTS

Many inexperienced navigators find two principal problems arise with sextant sight taking. Firstly, it can be difficult to hold the sextant still while the boat is moving in a seaway, and secondly, it can be difficult to find the heavenly body in the sextant telescope and bring it down to the horizon.

The first problem can only be overcome by practice. It is best to find a spot somewhere around the boat where the rigging or rails can provide support or bracing, then ask the helmsman to hold the boat as steady on course as possible. The sun is easier to use than stars or planets, so practice should be undertaken during the day rather than in the evening.

The procedure for finding the heavenly body in the telescope and bringing it down to the horizon also requires much practice. The usual procedure is as follows (the sun is used as an example, but the principle is the same for all bodies):

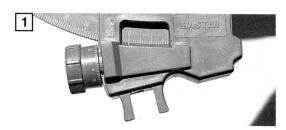

1. Set the sextant reading at zero on both the arc and the micrometer screw.

2. Set plenty of shades or you'll damage your eyes. Then point the sextant at the sun. There should be two suns, one in each side of the index mirror.

3. Release the clamp on the index arm and slowly bring the sextant down, all the time holding the reflected sun in the telescope by adjusting the index arm. The other sun will disappear out the top of the mirror.

4. Continue lowering until the horizon appears in the telescope. Release the clamp.

5. Adjust the micrometer screw to 'land' the sun on the horizon in the centre of the mirror.

6. This is the ideal situation for sight taking.

PRECISION SIGHT TAKING

As a general rule, the lower limb (LL) of the sun is taken, as sight corrections in the Nautical Almanac are based on this. (The lower limb of the sun is its bottom edge, normally used for sextant readings.)

If the upper limb (top edge) is taken, a correction must then be made. This is found in the relevant pages in the Nautical Almanac.

Positioning the sun on the horizon

Too high   *Too low*   *Just right*

The upper limb (UL) is more difficult to use because it requires more corrections and is therefore rarely used, although under certain circumstances it may be necessary to use this upper limb.

ROCKING THE SEXTANT

Since the angle measured by the sextant between the horizon and the sun is the vertical angle, the sextant must be absolutely vertical when the reading is taken. Short of fitting a spirit level to the sextant, this can be difficult to judge, but a neat navigator's trick provides an easy solution.

When the sun is touching the horizon, gently rock the sextant from side to side in the vertical plane. The sun will appear to rise up off the horizon, first to one

Below *As the sextant is tilted from side to side (rocked), the sun appears to rise first to one side and then the other. When it is at the bottom of the arc and in the centre of the mirror, the sextant is vertical and sights can be taken.*

side then the other. When it touches the horizon at the bottom of this arc, just like the bubble in a spirit level, the sextant is exactly vertical and the sight reading can be taken. If the reading is taken when the sun is to either side it will not be accurate. The same procedure is followed with a star, planet or the moon.

Left *Because of its shape, often only the upper limb (UL) of the moon is in a position to be brought down to the horizon. In this case the corrections must be read off for that situation.*

Below *Radio time signals ensure that nothing more than a reliable wrist watch is needed, providing accurate Universal Time (UT) is maintained.*

THE CHRONOMETER

The chronometer is an important part of the celestial navigator's equipment. So important was it in the days when ships often had no contact with the shore for weeks – even months – that the ship's chronometer was revered like a newborn baby. It was protected from heat and cold by insulation, swung in gymbals (levelling devices) to counter the movement of the ship, and even wound with a precise number of turns of the key at exactly the same time each day!

The reason for all this pampering was simple: if the chronometer developed any error the whole navigation of the ship was at risk.

Even one second of time could make a considerable difference to the outcome of celestial sights – the sun moves around the earth at a rate of about 1000 miles per hour (1609km per hour), so inaccuracy of even one second of time will make a big difference! Indeed, the invention of the chronometer was a major breakthrough in navigation.

Nowadays, modern radio communication avoids the need for such coddling; regular radio time signals ensure that if the chronometer develops any errors, they can be immediately detected and corrected. Indeed, many small boat skippers do not install a chronometer, but use only a reliable watch, checked daily with radio time signals, to provide an accurate time for sight taking. UT (Universal Time), formerly known as GMT (Greenwich Mean Time), is the world time, and is the key to accurate navigation. The taking of sextant sights must be timed exactly so that the position of the sun in the sky is known at the time the sight was taken.

The Nautical Almanac lists the position of the sun and other heavenly bodies used for navigation at any given time of UT on every day of the year. These form the basis of all celestial sights.

Radio time signals are broadcast on short wave from different parts of the world throughout the day and night, so there should be no difficulty in checking the boat's time piece – whatever it may be – at regular intervals. Details of where and when the time signals are broadcast are carried in the official international publication 'Radio Navigational Aids'.

However, occasionally radio problems can arise in the middle of the ocean, so a cautious skipper will 'rate' his chronometer by keeping a regular check on how much it gains or loses each day. Then if by some mischance radio time signals are not available, the rate factor can be applied to maintain accurate time on the chronometer.

The components of a towed log

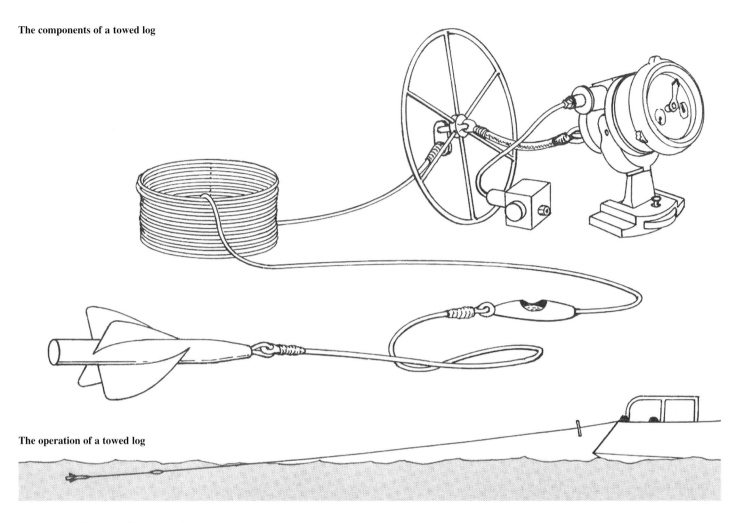

The operation of a towed log

THE DISTANCE LOG

Another important part of the navigator's equipment, the distance log measures the distance the boat travels through the water.

Most logs also incorporate measurement of speed, but as a general rule, navigation is concerned with the distance the boat has travelled rather than its speed. However, some modern electronic logs can be programmed to provide the distance travelled from the measurement of the boat's speed through the water.

The term 'log' comes from the days of slow sailing ships when the speed of the vessel was measured by throwing a log over the bow and recording the time it took to reach the stern. Because he knew the length of the ship, the navigator could then calculate the ship's speed.

The towed log

This type of log was used for many years by both large ships and boats, but it is rather cumbersome and has been mostly superseded by electronic logs, although some yacht owners still consider it useful.

It consists of a long, specially woven rope with a torpedo-like impeller (a small propeller driven by the passing flow of water) at the end, which is towed behind the boat. The impeller turns as it is pulled through the water, twisting the rope and recording the speed and distance on a dial fitted to the transom (stern) of the boat.

Despite its somewhat primitive operating system, the towed log, or Walker log, is surprisingly accurate. It is particularly good for yachts, as it is not affected by the heel of the boat, as is the case with some log units fitted under the hull.

Above *A towed (Walker) log. The inconvenience of streaming out and pulling in the long line with the impeller on the end makes it less popular than other logs. The dial is usually mounted on the stern rail.*

Above *The distance the boat travels is a vital factor in fixing its position at sea. This distance is needed to find the DR (Dead Reckoning) position and for use in sight calculations, so a reliable log is an important navigational instrument.*

The impeller log

This is based on the same principle as the towed log, but is more convenient as it is located beneath the hull and avoids having to 'stream' the log line each time the boat commences or ends a passage. A smaller, neater impeller turns as the boat moves through the water, indicating speed and distance on a dial in the cockpit or over the navigator's table.

The electromagnetic log

An electromagnetic log involves a magnetic sensor mounted on the outside of the hull or projected through it. The sensor is an induction device that produces a signal voltage, which varies with the speed of the hull through the water. A magnetic field in the water senses the speed through the water and transmits it to a readout in the cockpit.

The sonic speed sensor

This is similar in principle to the electromagnetic log but uses a sound beam transmitted through the water rather than a magnetic field. The sound is reflected against particles in the water as they pass the sensors, which analyze the echoes and measure the time it takes for the particles to pass. This time is converted to speed and recorded on a dial or display in the cockpit.

The measurement of distance on the log is given in nautical miles (one minute of latitude) and the measurement of speed in knots: one nautical mile per hour = one knot.

The term 'knot' is another traditional name that originated in the days of slow sailing ships. A triangular-shaped piece of timber on the end of a line (to create resistance to the water and hold it in position)

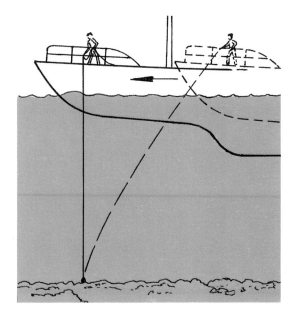

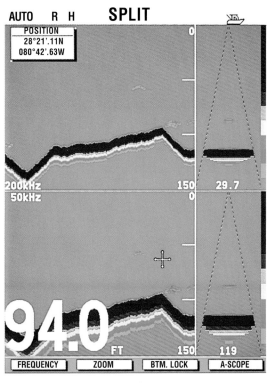

AUTO R H **SPLIT**

POSITION
28°21'.11N
080°42'.63W

200kHz 150 29.7
50kHz 0

94.0 FT 150 119

FREQUENCY ZOOM BTM. LOCK A-SCOPE

Far left *Lowering a leadline to the bottom to find the depth of water is still a good system for small boats in shallow water. The lead is thrown ahead of the boat and the depth measurement read as the boat passes over it.*

Left *The display of an electronic sounder not only provides the depth of water but also draws a picture of the sea bed contours. Some are sufficiently sensitive to register fish beneath the boat.*

was dropped over the stern on the end of a line and the ship sailed away from it. As the rope was paid out, knots tied at specific intervals along the line were counted and the speed of the ship measured by the number of knots paid out in a given time.

Although modern speed logs are far removed from these basic origins, the original terms 'log' and 'knot' have survived.

THE DEPTH SOUNDER

On the chart, the depth of water at any given point is known as the 'sounding', and the instruments used to determine the depth are known as 'sounders'.

The most basic – and traditional – sounder consists of a lead-weighted line with depths marked on it. The lead is dropped to the bottom and the depth measured from the mark on the line at sea level.

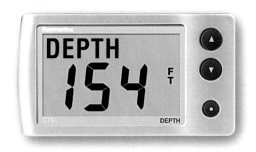

DEPTH **154** F T

Although still used by some small craft skippers, basic sounders have mostly been replaced by more sophisticated instruments known as 'depth sounders' or 'fish finders', which electronically 'bounce' a sound wave off the sea bed.

A transducer in the bottom of the hull transmits a series of sound waves directly downward which strike the sea bed and 'echo' back where they are picked up by the transducer. The time taken for the echo to return to the ship is electronically measured and indicates the depth of water beneath the hull, usually on an LC (liquid crystal) display over the navigator's table or in the cockpit.

Today's sounders are inexpensive, relatively small and very sophisticated – so much so, in fact, that they can even register schools of fish swimming under the boat. The depths can be read off a digital readout or presented as a contour of the sea bed on a display screen in full colour.

In the more advanced sounders the beam can be directed to the side or ahead of the boat, thus providing an electronic picture of the sea bed virtually all around the hull.

Left *Some electronic depth sounders indicate on a digital readout the depth of water beneath the hull.*

Harbour Navigation

Arguably the trickiest of all waterways in which to navigate are the enclosed waters of rivers, estuaries and harbours. Because most are sheltered and unaffected by the big seas and strong winds of the open sea, they give an often-misguided feeling of security and safety. Yet these seemingly benign waters can create more dangers for boat owners than the open stretches of coastline outside the entrance.

Statistically, far more small craft come to grief in sheltered waters than in the open sea. Indeed, experienced sailors caught out off the coast in a sudden blow will head out to sea rather than attempt to run into shelter; with a sound boat and an experienced crew, the risks of riding it out in open water are far less than attempting to negotiate the often dangerous entrance to a safe port.

Even when inside the protective arms of a harbour, the dangers are still high. If an anchor drags, there is the looming danger of a lee shore or an unpleasant reef close at hand. Similarly, there is little room to manoeuvre when caught in a tidal rip in a narrow channel – not to mention, of course, the hazards of waterborne traffic.

The navigator needs to be very aware of all the hazards associated with manoeuvring the vessel in and around a harbour or estuary, and even more so in a river. Big harbours used by commercial shipping will have at least the main channels marked with buoys and beacons, and often non-commercial waterways used extensively by boats will be well marked as well. But the more remote coastal regions have bays and

Opposite *The harbour entrance is the demarcation point between two very different forms of navigation – pilotage and coastal.*

inlets, rivers and estuaries that carry little or no markings and are familiar only to locals. It is in these waterways that the navigator's skill is tested to the full.

TIDES AND TIDAL STREAMS

One of the major problems encountered by navigators in harbours and estuaries is the tidal flow and its rise and fall. But while both can have a profound effect on safe pilotage, both are carefully monitored and should not create undue problems for experienced navigators, except where tidal phenomena are encountered.

Below Two important instruments for harbour navigation: the depth sounder (left) and the chart plotter (right).

HOW TIDES ARE CREATED

Seventy one percent of the earth's surface is covered by salt water. Due to a number of factors – notably the rotation of the earth and the gravitational effect of the sun and moon – this water is constantly moving. Every ocean has a circulating current around its perimeter, and sometimes (as in the Gulf Stream) across the centre (see Crossing the Oceans).

The twice-daily rise and fall of the tide occurs as a result of a tidal wave. The term 'tidal wave' has mistakenly become associated with the giant wave often seen in Hollywood movies, which in fact is a tsunami. The true tidal wave is much less dramatic. It is formed partly by earth's rotation and partly by the pull of the moon's and sun's gravity, and compared to a tsunami is relatively low in height with a very long wavelength.

When the combined gravitational effect of the sun and moon pull on the water surrounding the earth, it creates a pile-up of water in the form of a long wave that, as the earth rotates, travels around the globe. When this tidal wave strikes a coastline, the water level rises and then falls as the wave passes on, creating the cycle of high and low tides.

A second wave on the opposite side of the globe to the main tidal wave is created by the centrifugal force of the earth spinning, so that in fact two tidal waves travel around the world each day, causing two high and two low tides to occur. Where a coastline faces the open ocean with no major islands, shoals or other impediments offshore, the tides are easy to predict, with an even, twice-a-day cycle as the two waves go past.

Where there are offshore archipelago or constrictions that interfere with the flow of the wave, tides can develop strange movements.

In Southampton Water, England, for example, there are four tides a day, due to the tidal wave being broken in two by the Isle of Wight.

In some bottleneck waterways, such as the Bay of Fundy, Canada, the high tide can be held back to create incredible highs and then drop to equally remarkable lows. The interference of the Indonesian Archipelago creates a tidal phenomenon across

Right The water surrounding the earth is pulled up into a bulge by the gravitational attraction of the moon and, to a lesser extent, the sun. As this tidal wave tracks around the earth it creates high and low tides as it passes each coastline.

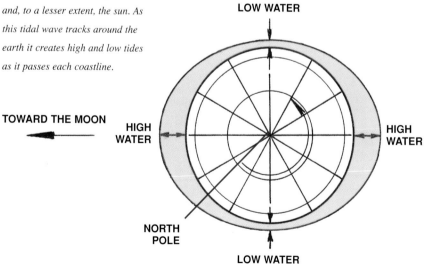

Northern Australia where frequently a high tide of 10m (32.8ft) is followed by the coastal sea bed drying out for some kilometres offshore, leaving vessels stranded. It is in such areas that the navigator must be fully aware of tidal phenomena that can place the vessel in danger.

SPRING AND NEAP TIDES

When the sun and moon are on opposite sides of the earth (full moon) or on the same side (new moon), their combined gravitational effect piles up the greatest amount of water, creating the largest tidal wave each month. When this tidal wave reaches coastal waterways, it causes a very high tide followed by a very low tide – the 'Spring Tide'.

When the sun and moon are pulling across one another (first and final quarters of the moon), the tidal wave is much lower, creating a low high water and a high low water, known as the 'Neap Tide'. Since the

movements of sun and moon are known, it is easy to accurately predict ahead what tides may be experienced, and this is the basis on which tide tables are drawn up.

As described earlier (page 40), the even rise and fall of the tide twice daily will exist only where the tidal wave has free access to the coastline. Where local phenomena interfere with the flow, their effect will change the tidal cycle. In much the same way, tidal predictions for different parts of a waterway can vary considerably.

At the mouth of a river estuary, for example, the time and height of the tides may be several hours different to the times and heights in the upper reaches.

All these factors are taken into consideration when compiling the official tide tables – one of the most important of all publications on board a boat.

Above *The most common cause of stranding is miscalculation of the tide.*

Below *Spring Tides are created with the sun and moon pulling in conjunction, and Neap Tides with the sun and moon pulling in opposition.*

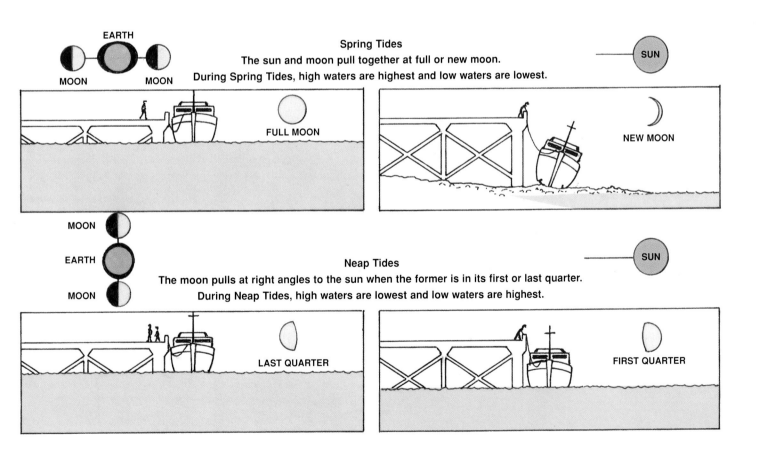

EARTH

MOON **MOON**

Spring Tides
The sun and moon pull together at full or new moon.
During Spring Tides, high waters are highest and low waters are lowest.

SUN

FULL MOON

NEW MOON

MOON

EARTH

MOON

Neap Tides
The moon pulls at right angles to the sun when the former is in its first or last quarter.
During Neap Tides, high waters are lowest and low waters are highest.

SUN

LAST QUARTER

FIRST QUARTER

TIDE TABLES

There is a wide range of tide tables available, from sponsored commercial pamphlets handed out as promotional material by fishing and boating enterprises to the official volumes issued by the authorities in each country around the world – mostly by the Hydrographic Office of the respective navy.

The official volumes, not surprisingly, are the most reliable, and these are available from most boat chandlers or nautical bookshops.

Local tide tables, issued by a selected state or local authority, may nevertheless also be useful, and they cover a specific port or waterway in more detail than the hydrographic office publications.

The layout of tide tables may vary a little, but most provide tidal predictions in two sections: major or standard ports and secondary ports.

The major ports are selected for their commercial importance or strategic location and their data is listed for every day of the year. Usually the local time (zone time) of the high and low waters is given, together with the depth in metres or feet above chart datum. Where the tide drops below chart datum the height is preceded by a minus sign.

It is important when using these tide tables to ensure that the correct time is used, taking into account Summer Time or any other local (zone) time adjustment.

The secondary ports section is not usually listed every day, but as a correction to be applied to a nearby – specified – standard port. The correction is given for both time and tide height and an indication provided as to whether it is added to or subtracted from the standard port reading. In this way, the tidal predictions for most navigable waterways are listed conveniently in the one volume.

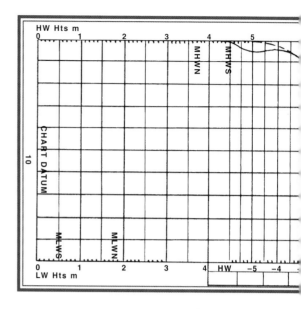

TIDAL STREAMS

The rise and fall of a tide is always accompanied by a surface movement of the water known as the tidal stream. This is mostly created by the flow of the incoming (flood) or outgoing (ebb) tide moving into or out of the waterway, but may be varied as it moves along channels and around obstructions. Where a bottleneck occurs, the water can pile up and create extremely fast tidal streams. One such phenomenon on the north coast of Australia is so dramatic that on either side of the bottleneck the sea is at considerably different levels, creating a mill race that is picturesquely described as a 'horizontal waterfall'! However, these are extremes and most tidal streams are moderate, although often still significant enough to cause serious problems of navigation unless they are understood and countered.

While tidal flows can be charted, as is the case in some major areas such as the English Channel, the topographical features of a local waterway can affect the tidal flow. For example, the flood tide in an estuary can be affected at different times of the day, even the month, by the runout of the river water, and can also vary at different points as well as at different states of the river. For these waterways, local information is essential and a wise navigator will make a point of contacting the local authorities to obtain information about any local tidal phenomena

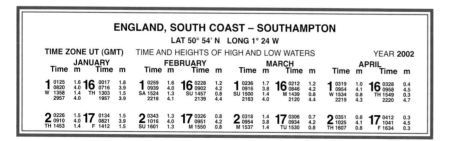

ENGLAND, SOUTH COAST – SOUTHAMPTON

LAT 50° 54' N LONG 1° 24' W

TIME ZONE UT (GMT)   TIME AND HEIGHTS OF HIGH AND LOW WATERS   YEAR **2002**

	JANUARY				FEBRUARY				MARCH				APRIL		
Time	m	Time	m	Time	m	Time	m	Time	m	Time	m	Time	m	Time	m
1 0125 0820 W 1358 2957	1.6 4.0 1.4 4.0	**16** 0017 0716 TH 1303 1957	1.8 3.9 1.5 3.9	**1** 0259 0939 SA 1524 2216	1.6 4.0 1.3 4.1	**16** 0228 0902 SU 1457 2139	1.2 4.2 0.8 4.4	**1** 0236 0916 SU 1500 2163	1.7 3.8 1.4 4.0	**16** 0212 0846 M 1439 2120	1.2 4.2 0.8 4.4	**1** 0319 0954 W 1534 2219	1.0 4.1 0.8 4.3	**16** 0328 0958 TH 1549 2220	0.4 4.5 0.3 4.7
2 0226 0910 TH 1453	1.5 4.0 1.4	**17** 0134 0821 F 1412	1.5 3.9 1.5	**2** 0343 1016 SU 1601	1.3 4.0 1.3	**17** 0326 0951 M 1550	0.8 4.2 0.8	**2** 0318 0954 M 1537	1.4 3.8 1.4	**17** 0306 0934 TU 1530	0.7 4.2 0.8	**2** 0351 1025 TH 1607	0.8 4.1 0.8	**17** 0412 1041 F 1634	0.3 4.5 0.3

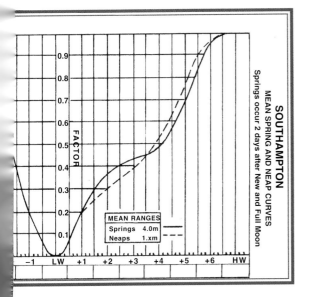

SOUTHAMPTON
MEAN SPRING AND NEAP CURVES
Springs occur 2 days after New and Full Moon

MEAN RANGES
Springs 4.0m
Neaps   1.xm

that may affect his vessel on entering a port. This is particularly important when crossing a bar at the entrance to a river or estuary, where a safe crossing may only be possible at a certain state of the tide.

THE 'RULE OF TWELFTHS'

When navigating in a harbour or other restricted waterway, it is sometimes necessary to find the height or flow of the tide in-between the times of high and low water given in the tide tables. A rough rule of thumb used by navigators works on the assumption that the tide changes height by one-twelfth of its full height in the first hour after high or low water. It changes two-twelfths in the second hour, three twelfths in the third and fourth hours, two-twelfths in the fifth hour and one-twelfth in the sixth hour. The sequence can be remembered as: 1-2-3-3-2-1.

From this an idea of the rate of flow of the tide as well as the height at times between the top and bottom of the tide can be determined.

Apart from information obtained from tide tables and local authorities, the Sailing Directions or Pilots contain general tidal information and details of any tidal phenomenon and should be consulted when entering a port.

The chart may also provide information in the form of current arrows indicating the direction and flow rate of flood and ebb tides. On the chart an arrow with

half feathers indicates the direction of the flow during flood tide and an arrow without feathers indicates the flow of ebb tides. The approximate speed of the tidal flow is given alongside the arrows.

BUOYS AND BUOYAGE

Most estuaries, harbours and rivers contain hazards that are a threat to safe navigation. They can range from less visible things such as shoal patches, sunken reefs or tide rips to more tangible features such as water traffic, especially commercial vessels.

Most ports have local rules and regulations and navigators should familiarize themselves with these as well as any sailing directions which are relevant. Navigating in a strange harbour is akin to driving in a strange city; care and caution are required or a pleasant visit can turn into a major nightmare.

To assist navigation, port authorities provide guidance in the form of buoys, beacons and other markers at strategic points. Some of these may be local markers, but in most harbours of any substance, an international system is used.

Some markers may be located on the shore, some on beacons or buoys in the water. Most use colours to identify them and assist in interpretation of the danger they mark, while shapes – mostly in the form of topmarks – are also used. Lights on these markers provide guidance at night.

Bottom *A page from a Tidal Stream Atlas. Note that there is a page for each hour of the tidal cycle, indicating direction and strength of tidal streams.*

Below *Buoys come in many shapes, sizes and colours, with different topmarks, all of which are designed to indicate to the navigator factors that might affect the safety of the vessel.*

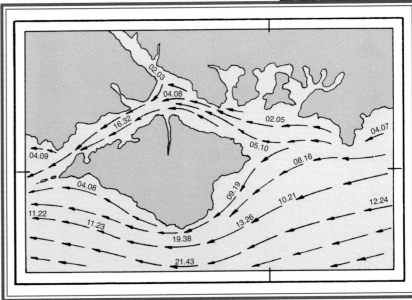

The Lateral System

Lateral buoys and beacons are the marks that are used to indicate a channel or safe water. The term 'lateral' means 'to the side', and when applied to these marks the term indicates the side of the boat on which they must be passed, although some mariners prefer the description that they indicate the side on which safe water lies.

Either way, where a channel is concerned, they mark the sides of the channel and when individual dangers are marked, the colour and shape of the buoy and its topmark indicate on which side the danger lies.

Strangely, the system of marking is not universal, and indeed the colours and shapes adopted in IALA Zone B are quite different and even opposite to those in IALA Zone A.

In both zones, red and green lateral buoys are used to mark channels, but in Zone A the red buoys indicate the port (left) side of the channel while in Zone B the red buoys indicate the starboard (right) side of the channel. The left and right side of the channel are determined by assuming the vessel is making into the harbour from seaward.

Thus the basic maxim for entering a harbour or a channel when coming in from sea is as follows:

IALA ZONE A

Keep red channel buoys and beacons to port and green to starboard.

IALA ZONE B

Keep green channel buoys and beacons to port and red to starboard.

Shapes and topmarks are also used to indicate the side on which lateral buoys must be passed. Port-hand buoys – to be passed on the port side – are usually can-shaped and if they carry topmarks these are also usually in the form of a can.

Starboard-hand buoys are mostly cone or 'nun'-shaped and carry a triangular topmark. The colour of the topmark and light, if shown, are the same colour as the buoy they surmount, but will have different flashing characteristics to identify one from the other.

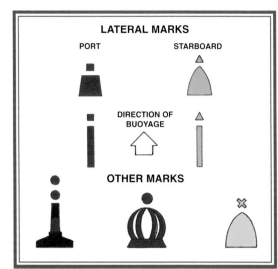

LATERAL MARKS

PORT   STARBOARD

DIRECTION OF
BUOYAGE

OTHER MARKS

ISOLATED DANGER MARKS

As the name indicates, these are buoys or beacons indicating an isolated danger such as a reef or sandbank in the middle of a waterway. They usually take the form of a buoy or a pile (a post driven into the sea bed) situated on the hazard and unless otherwise indicated, can be passed on either side.

Colours may vary, but black and red horizontal stripes are a popular colour pattern, while topmarks, if any, consist of two black balls, one above the other; any light carried is white.

SAFE WATER MARKS

Once again, the name says it all. Safe water marks, which may be buoys, beacons or piles, indicate that safe water lies all around and they can therefore be passed on either side. They are painted with red and white vertical stripes and show a white light at night.

OTHER MARKS

It is often necessary to place a warning buoy or beacon in places where the normal IALA system does not suit – a diver-training area, for example, or a restricted naval zone. Details of the marks and lights used for these will be carried on the chart and in the Sailing Directions.

Above and opposite right
Buoys are not only numbered for identification on the chart – many of them are named instead.

Left *Piles or beacons in shallow water have the same lights and marks as equivalent buoys.*

Above Ocean lights have powerful beams and use white lights, which have a greater range than coloured lights.

Below Common light cycles for navigation lights and beacons: a combination of flashes and time cycles makes identification of each individual light quite simple (see panel, right).

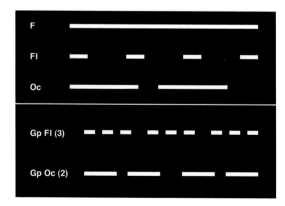

confusion the navigator is able to identify the lights necessary for piloting the boat, a system of colours and characteristics has been developed and is used in almost all waterways of the world.

LIGHT CHARACTERISTICS

Other than in exceptional cases, white, red and green are the only colours used for navigation lights. This is rather limiting, though, so it is necessary to provide additional means of identifying navigation lights. This is done by varying the flashing characteristic of the light. The following are the main characteristics used and the abbreviation that they are given on the chart:

LIGHTS AND LIGHTHOUSES

Lighthouses are the mariner's signposts and are located at strategic points along the coastline, at the entrance to ports and in harbours, estuaries and rivers. Most of the big coastal lights are white, with flashing characteristics, but in harbours and estuaries a wide range of colours and characteristics are used, for these lights are more numerous than offshore lights and have more specific tasks to do.

Harbour lights may be placed on the shoreline, on background hills, on bridges, buildings, buoys and beacons. They may be used for plotting the boat's position on the chart, depending on the size of the waterway, but they are most often used for visual navigation. Some are even designed to visually guide boats through tricky passages and winding channels.

In a busy harbour there can be literally dozens of navigation lights, to say nothing of the plethora of shore lights around the perimeter of the waterway. Since it is vitally important that from all this

LIGHT SIGNALS

F	Fixed light – Remains constant; does not flash or occult.
Q	Quick flashing – 50–60 per minute.
Fl	Flashing – The period of light is shorter than the period of darkness.
GpFl	Group flashing – The light flashes in groups, usually of two, three or four flashes.
Oc	Occulting – The period of light is longer than the period of darkness.
GpOc	Group occulting – Occulting in groups, usually two, three or four occultations.
Iso	Isophase – The period of light is the same as the period of darkness.
Alt	Alternating – The flashes are in alternating colours.

To further identify the light, its characteristic may be given a time cycle:

GpFl(2) 10 secs – the light will flash in groups of two flashes with a 10-second cycle. (The cycle is from the beginning of the first flash in the first group to the beginning of the first flash in the second group.)

SECTORED LIGHTS

Some lights in and around harbours, particularly near the entrance, are so situated that they provide a guidance system for vessels moving into the waterway or along its channels. One system uses what is known as a 'sectored' light, in which different colours are used to indicate the boat's position in relation to a channel or danger. To achieve this, the light is divided into sectors, each showing an individual colour. As the boat passes from one sector into another, the colour of the light changes, giving some indication of the vessel's position.

A typical use for a sectored light is at the entrance to a harbour. The light is located behind the entrance in such a position that it shines directly out to sea. The middle sector shows a white light directly through the entrance. The sector covering the left headland (seen from seaward) is red and the sector covering the right headland, green. Thus, a vessel making into port from seaward needs only to stay in the white light to make a safe entrance.

If the light changes to red, the boat is too far to the left of the channel, and if it goes green, the boat is too much to the right. By staying in the white sector the vessel will sail right through the centre of the entrance channel.

Sectored lights are also used to warn of isolated dangers. If a light is sectored so that the red sector of the light shines over a dangerous reef or shoal, navigators will know that when they see the red light they are getting into a dangerous position (the nautical term is 'standing into danger') and must change course until the vessel is back in the white sector.

Above *The rotating beam of a powerful navigation light appears as a brilliant flash when the beam passes over the boat.*

Left *This illustrates the way in which a sectored light covers a coastal hazard, where colours are used to indicate the boat's position in relation to danger.*

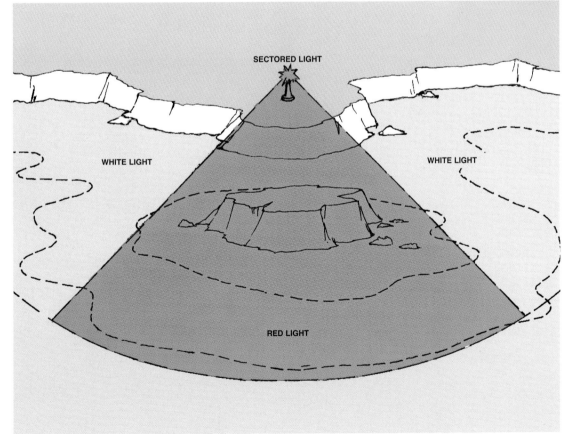

SECTORED LIGHT

WHITE LIGHT

WHITE LIGHT

RED LIGHT

LEAD LIGHTS OR RANGE LIGHTS

This is another system of guidance that uses lights or shapes. It is more precise than the sectored light system and is commonly used in narrow channels or rivers where the vessel needs to be held on an exact course.

The system uses two lights – one located above the other and some distance behind it. These two lights are so arranged that when they are one above the other, as seen from the boat, they indicate the centre of the channel. A vessel making along a channel will line up the two lights and then steer towards them, keeping both exactly one above the other. If the lower light moves to the right of the upper light the boat is drifting to the left of the channel, and if the lower light moves to the left of the upper light, the vessel is drifting to the right.

Using a series of these lead lights, boats can be guided along twisting channels, around dangers, even into locks or canals. A series of lead lights, usually located on the shore at strategic points, enables the navigator to move from one channel into the next as each new set of lights comes into line.

In daylight a similar system is used where the lights are replaced by coloured triangular shapes; the lower pointing upwards and the upper inverted. The boat is in the exact centre of the channel when the tips of the two triangles are touching.

Above and right *At night, lead lights are aligned in the same way as the beacons during the day.*

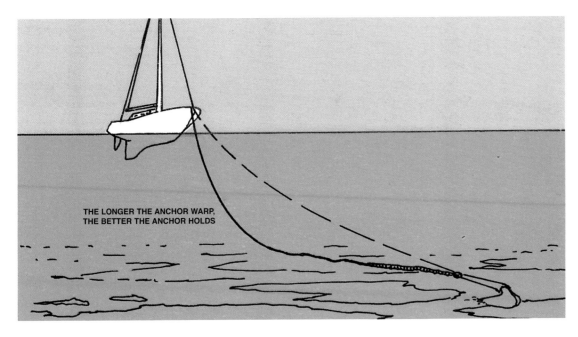

Left It is common to let out the
anchor warp to about five to
seven times the depth of water.
However, much will depend on
the nature of the sea bed and
weather conditions.

THE LONGER THE ANCHOR WARP,
THE BETTER THE ANCHOR HOLDS

ANCHORING

Almost every boat that enters a harbour will at some
stage come to anchor. While this is generally a fairly
simple exercise, it can be fraught with problems
unless care is taken, not only with the anchoring procedure but also in preparation. The following is a general guide to the steps that should be taken when
anchoring in an unfamiliar waterway:

- Check with the local authorities for any restrictions
  on anchoring in any particular
  areas of the harbour.
- Check the Sailing Directions or
  any local publication to determine
  the tidal conditions that exist.
  Avoid strong tidal flows.
- Find out what the prevailing bad
  weather winds are and select a
  comfortable spot under a lee.
- Study the chart and ensure that the
  selected spot has a good holding
  ground with no lee shore or other
  dangers nearby.
- Check for dangers such as sub-
  marine or overhead cables or
  prohibited anchorage zones.

- Determine the depth of water and calculate a safe
  length of anchor warp to let out.
- When the boat has brought up to the anchor, take a
  full fix position by Global Positioning System
  (GPS) or cross bearings and mark this on the chart.
- Select two sets of transits, at right angles if possible, so any signs of the anchor dragging will be
  immediately obvious.

Below Transit bearings are
ideal for visual checking that
the anchor is not dragging.
Ideally, the two transits should
be 90° apart, or as close as
possible to this angle.

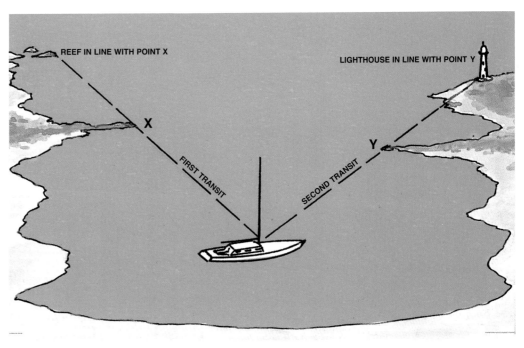

REEF IN LINE WITH POINT X

LIGHTHOUSE IN LINE WITH POINT Y

X

Y

FIRST TRANSIT

SECOND TRANSIT

Below right *Provided they are both marked on the chart, the church and the lighthouse make an ideal transit bearing.*

Below *Stocking up for an ocean passage is known as 'vittling', after the old sailors' term for food – 'vittles'.*

DEPARTURE AND ARRIVAL PROCEDURES

Since there is a distinct demarcation between navigation in the open sea and harbour navigation, there needs to be a point outside every harbour where the sea passage begins and ends.

These are known as Departure and Arrival Positions and are entered in the log book as such. It is one of the navigator's responsibilities to establish these positions for future reference in the event of a mishap during the passage. Preparation for an offshore passage does not simply involve putting aboard the necessary stores; nor does arrival mean just tying up to a vacant wharf. The skipper and crew will have plenty to do getting the boat shipshape, but the busiest person on board is always the navigator.

DEPARTURE

The first stop for the navigator, when preparing to leave port, will be the marina bookshop or chandlers to pick up any relevant charts and sailing directions for the approaching passage.

Of prime importance are the Notices to Mariners, which contain any changes to charts or publications and any warnings of new dangers either on the passage or at the arrival port. Having collected all the paperwork, the navigator will then set to and correct the charts and publications and note any anomalies or changes that may affect the passage. Obviously this is also the time to replace any equipment that is worn, particularly 2B pencils and other chart instruments.

The next step is to check and calibrate the navigation equipment. It is unlikely that the compass will need to be swung unless some major work has been

carried out on the boat or a great deal of canned stores are creating a magnetic anomaly below decks. However, it is always wise to check the compass by lining the boat up on a transit bearing to see that no major problem, such as a needle dropping off, has occurred.

The GPS should be checked by taking it to the nearest checking point marked on the chart, and similarly, any other electronic gear should be checked out and the batteries examined to see that they are in good condition and the electrolyte levels are topped up. If the passage is to be lengthy or across an ocean, the sextant and other celestial navigation requirements must be checked.

When the boat clears the harbour entrance the Departure Position must be established. This is the point on which all navigation on the passage will be based. A positive position fix, either by GPS or cross bearings, must be plotted on the chart, at which point the boat's head is swung onto the first course and the log started.

An entry in the log book giving the time and the latitude and longitude of the Departure Position is an important legal requirement and makes the first log book entry for the passage.

ARRIVAL

If the boat is arriving from overseas it will be necessary to make contact by radio with the harbour master and other authorities, such as quarantine and immigration officials.

If the passage has been along the home coast, the only call need be to the harbour master.

The harbour master will provide information on navigating the entrance to the harbour, the condition of the bar (if there is one), tidal details and any special port rules. Indeed, it is part of the job to ensure that the skipper and navigator are informed of anything that may create problems for the incoming vessel.

Before entering the harbour, the Arrival Position is plotted on the chart and then entered in the log book, as with the Departure Position. From here in navigation will almost certainly be visual.

Above Even big ocean liners need careful preparation before departure on an extended passage. This is equally important with small vessels.

Left Safe arrival is the happy outcome of careful preparation, good seamanship and accurate navigation.

COASTAL
NAVIGATION

Between its Departure Position outside one port and its Arrival Position at the next, your boat or craft will be in the open sea. If this passage involves heading across a long stretch of water out of sight of land for some time, then there's no doubt that you will require celestial or electronic navigation skills. If the coastline will be visible for most of the passage, coastal navigation is what you'll need, where the boat's progress will be tracked by means of visual sightings of land objects.

In essence, then, coastal navigation is navigation in sight of land, but there will be occasions when coastal navigation can be used even when no land is in sight. When crossing a wide estuary or indentation in the coastline, for example, coastal navigation can be used by means of dead, or deduced, reckoning (estimating how far the boat has progressed along its course – see page 59) or transferred bearing procedures.

Basic navigation equipment and basic navigation techniques are all that is required to navigate along a coastal stretch. A sextant is not necessary, although it can be used, as there are no involved mathematical calculations and little need to consult tables. With coastal navigation, most tracking and plotting are done with the compass and log.

COASTAL CHARTS
For coastal navigation, the charts will be mainly medium to large scale: a medium-scale chart will cover most of the coastline between Departure and Arrival Positions; and a series of

Opposite *Because of their sophisticated power source, large yachts have the capacity to carry a wide range of the latest electronic equipment.*

large-scale charts will provide the fine detail of each segment of the coastline along the track.

If the passage is to be broken by a visit to a port along the way, or a stopover or two in a pleasant anchorage, then additional large-scale charts covering the port, or the anchorage area only, will also be necessary.

The choice of metric or fathom charts is not important, providing they are both reliable – the trend is toward metric (one fathom = six feet = 1.83m).

Coastal navigation is carried out almost entirely on the chart, so a good selection of charts, both official and privately published, should be on board. They should all be corrected for current Notices to Mariners (see page 17), Sailing Directions and other relevant publications from local authorities. Tide tables are essential, while tide charts can be useful. Parallel rules, a Portland plotter or a protractor, dividers, a pair of compasses and a 2B pencil are necessary to work on the charts.

In terms of instruments for coastal navigation, a steering compass, a hand-bearing compass and a distance log are essential. Many boats use a Global Positioning System (GPS), which is a satellite navigation system, for plotting a coastal passage (see Electronic Navigation, page 110).

LAYING OFF A STRAIGHT COURSE

To sail along a specified course from one point to another, the course must first be laid off (drawn) on the chart, corrected for compass error and transferred to the steering compass. By maintaining that course on the compass, the boat will travel along the set track.

- Establish on the chart the Departure and Arrival Positions.
- Check that no hazards lie along the route.
- Place the parallel rules so that one edge passes through both points. Draw a line along this edge to represent the track to be followed.
- Move the parallel rules across to the nearest compass rose until one edge runs through the centre.
- Draw a line along this edge from the centre of the compass rose to the perimeter in the direction the boat will head.
- Where this line cuts the outer edge of the compass rose, read off the true course to steer from departure to arrival positions.
- Apply compass error as described on pages 24–26. The result is the compass course to steer in order to follow the required track.
- Turn the boat until this heading appears against the lubber line on the steering compass.

Right *The course line is laid off on the chart and transferred to the nearest compass rose by means of parallel rules.*

Far right *The true course is read off the compass rose, corrected for compass error and written on the chart beside the course line. This is the course to steer.*

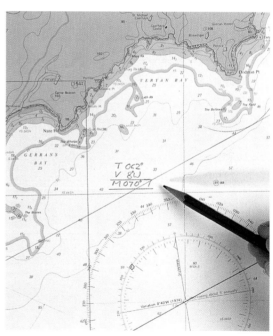

LAYING OFF A COMPLEX COURSE

Very rarely will the course from departure to arrival points be a straight line; it is more likely to circumvent headlands, or divert past islands, rocks and other usually known hazards.

When this occurs, planning the passage becomes a great deal more complex. The navigator must determine what he or she considers a safe distance to pass around each hazard, in fine weather as well as in bad conditions. The navigator must make allowances for the boat to be blown off course, or encounter an unexpected current or set, and try to predict any other problems that might arise and cause the boat to be pushed off course and into danger.

This is where the skill and experience of a navigator come into play. He or she must plan ahead to clear each hazard by a safe distance, and also anticipate any unforeseen event that could place the boat in danger.

Each hazard along the passage is examined and a safe distance to pass determined according to the time of day or night the boat will pass, and what adjustment might be necessary for any adverse conditions of wind or sea.

Once all these factors have been taken into consideration, the navigator will take a pair of compasses and, on the chart, draw a 'danger circle' around each hazard. The radius of that circle is the safe distance. By placing the point of the compasses on the outmost point of each danger and drawing a circle around it, the navigator can establish a series of 'danger circles'.

The procedure for laying off a complex course from departure to the arrival, which will pass a safe distance outside all hazards, is as follows:

- Lay the parallel rules onto the chart and draw a straight course from the Departure Position at a tangent to the first danger circle.
- Move the rules carefully across the chart and read off the true course from the nearest compass rose. Convert this to a compass course and mark it alongside the first course.
- Lay the parallel rules on the chart so that one edge lies at a tangent to the first danger circle and the same edge lies at a tangent to the second danger circle. Draw a line between these two tangents – this is the second leg of the course.

- Read off the true course from the compass rose and convert it to a compass course. Write it alongside the second course.
- Repeat the procedure with courses joining all the danger circles along the track, and write the relative compass course to steer alongside each leg of the track. Remember that deviation does not stay the same on each course.
- From a tangent to the final danger circle draw a straight line to the Arrival Position. This is the final leg of the passage.

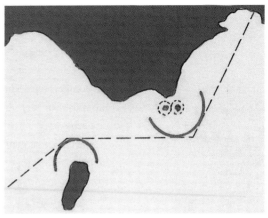

Above *A complex course is laid off as a series of tangents to danger circles.*

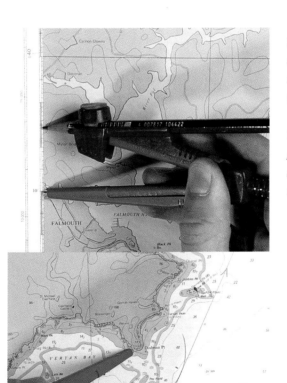

Left *To create a danger circle, a pair of compasses is set at the safe distance, measured from the latitude scale.*

Bottom left *From the outermost point of the danger, a circle is drawn around it. The vessel must not sail within this circle.*

TIME ON PASSAGE

In estimating the safe distance to pass each hazard, it is necessary to first estimate the time the boat will reach it, as obviously, a hazard that will be passed at night will need a greater clearance than one passed in daylight.

By setting the dividers at a suitable mileage on the latitude scale – five minutes (five nautical miles) would be suitable in most cases – the distance along the track to each alter-course point can be stepped off (measured along the course line with the dividers) and the time the boat will reach each point can be determined. Of course, this is more difficult with sailboats than with powerboats, because the strength and the direction of the wind will affect the boat's progress.

It is always convenient to know the approximate time of altering course at the end of each leg (the distance run between waypoints on a composite course), and also, by measuring along the full length of the passage, the estimated time of arrival at destination. In this way the navigator can provide an Estimated Time of Arrival (ETA) to the Coastguard and the Harbour Master at the arrival port.

While almost certainly the conditions of wind and sea will cause some changes to the estimated times, it is important for Search and Rescue (SAR) to receive this information in case some mishap occurs during the passage. Times can always be adjusted as the passage progresses.

LEEWAY

A number of factors affects a boat as she moves along her course line. The effect of stray offshore currents and streams is one, but this is almost impossible to estimate and, anyway, can only be found and countered as the boat progresses.

Another unknown factor – but a more estimable one – is leeway, which is the effect of the boat being pushed off course by the wind. This affects sailboats more than power craft because of the greater windage of the sails. Leeway can be estimated reasonably accurately by watching the amount the boat drifts off course under differing wind conditions. Most boat owners soon get to know how much leeway their boat makes by noting performance in varying wind strengths.

Like variation and deviation (refer to page 24), leeway is applied to the course before it is given to the helmsman.

Leeway can vary considerably from boat to boat: a big motor yacht may make only 5° of leeway while a similar-sized yacht might make 15°, depending on the wind conditions.

The number of degrees of leeway allowed is always applied to the course in the opposite direction to which the boat is drifting, just as the amount of set allowed is applied in the opposite direction in which the boat is being pushed.

Below *Leeway increases with the heel of the yacht, as the deep keel presents less lateral resistance to the water and the hull slides sideways.*

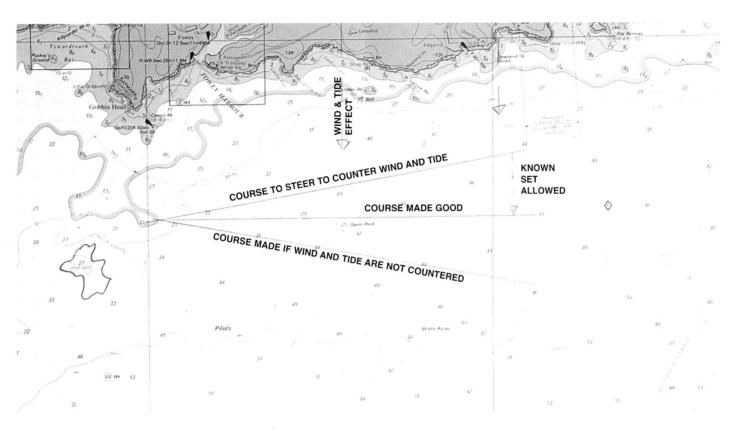

WIND & TIDE EFFECT

COURSE TO STEER TO COUNTER WIND AND TIDE

KNOWN SET ALLOWED

COURSE MADE GOOD

COURSE MADE IF WIND AND TIDE ARE NOT COUNTERED

SET

Two main factors, both of which are called 'set', influence the progress of the boat along the planned course line: one is called 'known set' and the other 'unknown set'.

Known set is the combination of known tidal or current influences that, like leeway, tend to push the boat off course. They can be calculated and applied before the passage begins. Unknown set comprises a variety of unpredictable factors that affect the boat but cannot be determined until the boat has progressed some way along her course line.

The direction and speed of a known set can be found either from the chart or from tidal publications and Sailing Directions. It is applied in the same way as leeway – into the set (in the opposite direction to which the set is running) to counter its effect.

However, the causes of the unknown set cannot be determined beforehand. These may be the result of bad steering, unexpected tidal flows, incorrect application of leeway or any other factor that affects the boat. Collectively they are termed 'unknown set' and

before they can be applied to the course the amount of this unknown set must be determined. Finding and counteracting an unknown set are described in detail on page 71.

DEAD RECKONING AND ESTIMATED POSITION

The most basic method of estimating a boat's position at any point is to measure the distance it has progressed along the course. This is known as the 'Dead (deduced) Reckoning' (DR) position and is obviously not entirely reliable, as any number of unknown factors will attempt to push it off course.

If any of these factors are known, or if they can be estimated – leeway or a known current, for example – they may be applied to give a more accurate position, known as an 'Estimated Position' (EP). Although possibly still not completely accurate, this is the most precise position that can be found without using position fixes. A DR position is indicated on the chart by a cross over the position; an EP by a triangle with a dot in the centre.

Above *Known set is the amount a boat is pushed off course by established wind and tide movement. To counteract it, the amount of set is applied to the course line into the direction from which it comes.*

COMPASS BEARINGS

As the boat progresses along its course, it is important to check on her position at regular intervals – the frequency of position fixing depends on the proximity of navigational dangers.

It is also important to keep a check on her progress so that alteration of course onto the next leg is done on time and on target. In coastal navigation these checks are mostly made by using shore objects to obtain 'fixes' of the boat's position; these fixes are plotted on the chart so that any drift is spotted immediately.

A number of instruments and techniques are used to make these checks, but by far the most common is the use of compass bearings.

The hand-bearing compass, generally used in preference to the steering compass, must be checked to ensure that superfluous errors do not creep in when it is used at different points around the boat.

Although most experienced navigators always use the hand-bearing compass from the same position (where any errors have been predetermined), this is not always possible – the shore object might be behind a sail or cabin structure, for example. A quick check is then necessary to ensure no errors have crept in. The procedure for taking a bearing of a shore object is described in Instruments and Aids in Navigation, page 23).

A bearing, or Line of Position (LOP), when transferred from the compass to the chart, indicates a line along which the position of the vessel is located. The compass is sighted onto the shore object and the compass reading taken off, then converted to a true bearing. The parallel rules are aligned with this bearing on the nearest compass rose and transferred across the chart, until one edge of the rule touches the shore object. A line drawn to seaward from the shore object represents the bearing, and the boat's position lies somewhere along that line.

Bearings are used for a number of purposes in plotting, such as to alter course.

BEAM BEARING

This is a bearing at 90° to the boat's course, which is particularly useful as it can be employed without using the compass.

A part of the vessel that runs across the deck from side to side at right angles to the boat's fore and aft line (the aft end of the cabin, for example) can be used to sight up beam bearings. When a shore object is in line with this and the boat is on course, the object lies on the beam bearing – useful for a number of plots and as an alter course bearing. The beam bearings of major shore objects are often entered in the logbook as they are passed, as a means of keeping a record of the passage.

Below left *Laying off a bearing on the chart: the bearing of an object taken from the compass is converted to true by applying the compass error, and then laid off on an adjacent compass rose.*

Below right *By transferring the true bearing from the compass rose across the chart until it runs to seaward from the object, a bearing or LOP of the object will be plotted on the chart. The boat lies somewhere along this line.*

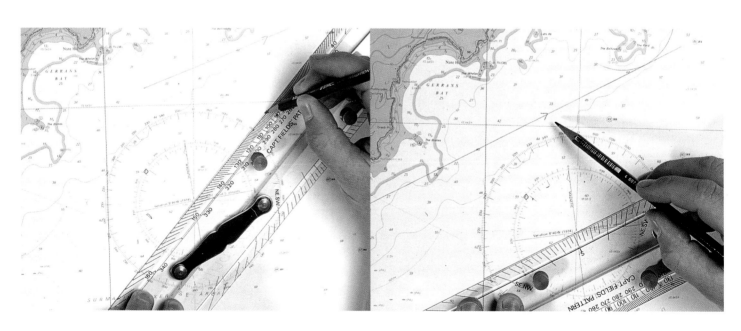

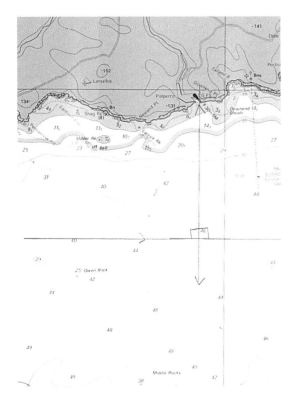

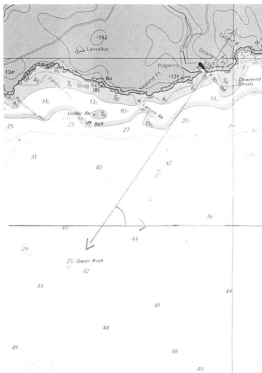

Far left *A beam bearing can be determined by sighting the shore object over a cross member of the boat's construction (such as the rear of the cabin top) when the boat is exactly on course, or it can be measured by taking a compass bearing at 90° to the boat's course.*

Left *A relative angle is the angle between the bearing of the object and the boat's heading. It is named port and starboard according to the side used – e.g. 30° to port.*

RELATIVE BEARING

This is a bearing relative to the boat's course – in other words, the number of degrees on either side of the bow. A beam bearing is a relative bearing because it is at 90° to the boat's course.

A bearing halfway between the bow and the beam would be a 45° relative bearing (to port or starboard as the case may be). Relative bearings are also used in plotting.

TRANSIT BEARING

The bearing provided by two objects in line is referred to as a transit bearing.

TRANSFERRED BEARING

A bearing can be transferred along the chart and used some distance from where it was taken, to provide part of a position fix. This is one of the most common methods of plotting the boat's position when only one object is in sight.

The technique used to take a transferred bearing is called the 'running fix'.

CROSSED BEARINGS

When a bearing is taken of a shore object, the position of a boat is known to lie somewhere along that bearing. If a bearing of another object is taken at the same time, the boat is known to lie somewhere along that bearing also – the only place the boat can then be is where the two bearings cross. This is the basis of many plotting fixes.

ALTERING COURSE ON A BEARING

The radius of a circle is at right angles to a tangent to that circle, so when using tangents to danger circles as part of a complex course, it is often convenient to use the beam bearing as the point at which to alter course.

Beam bearings are not the only bearings used for altering course, though. When approaching a point where the boat is to change onto a new course, a line is drawn on the chart from the alter course position to a prominent shore object and converted to a compass bearing. When the boat is on that bearing it is time to alter course.

PLOTTING

Plotting can be defined as establishing the boat's position on a chart as she makes her way along the track. In coastal navigation this usually involves taking a series of fixes using compass bearings of visual objects on shore. These need not necessarily be navigation marks or objects, although lighthouses and the like are easiest to use and are often strategically placed along the coastline.

Any object that is prominent enough to provide a good compass bearing and is marked on the chart is suitable for plotting purposes: a church steeple or readily identifiable building, a small island or even a distinctive cliff face. Mountain tops, because they are often rounded and far away, are not so good, and sand hills or low, scrubby foreshores rarely provide good points for taking bearings.

TAKING BEARINGS

First step in using bearings to establish a fix of the boat's position, as explained earlier, is to select objects that can be easily seen and identified. Second step is actually taking the bearings – and in practice this can require a degree of expertise.

The problem arises mainly because of the movement in the compass card, and it is here that the quality of the hand-bearing compass comes into play. Because it is balanced on a pivot, the compass card is free to swing easily, and if it is not well built and well damped, it will swing all over the place. Not even the best helmsman can hold a small yacht steady in a seaway (the movement of water created by the waves) and as a result, taking bearings can be very difficult indeed: the card will almost certainly be swinging wildly as the bearing is taken.

If the card is well damped, it is often possible to average out the swing on either side of the lubber line and obtain a reasonably accurate bearing. Even so, a number of attempts should be made before the reading is accepted as accurate. A good practice is to have a colleague stand by with a pencil to jot down a series of readings called out by the navigator; from these an average should provide a reasonably accurate reading.

The problem is exacerbated when wind and weather deteriorate, when the object is a long way off or difficult to sight over the compass, and at night, when there is a mere pinpoint of light that disappears regularly as the light flashes on and off. However well braced, the navigator is going to have his or her work cut out in maintaining a balance and footing!

__Opposite__ Sailing close inshore calls for accurate navigation, as there can be many hazards here that do not exist in deeper water.

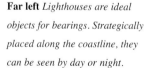

__Far left__ Lighthouses are ideal objects for bearings. Strategically placed along the coastline, they can be seen by day or night.

__Left__ The hand-bearing compass is a useful navigational instrument when making coastal passages. It can be carried around the boat until a convenient position is found, with good visibility of the shoreline.

63

THE FIXES

Once a series of bearings has been taken and the most accurate result obtained, these bearings must be converted to true bearings and plotted on the chart.

One bearing will not give a fix by itself because, as already indicated, the position of the boat lies somewhere along the bearing, but there is no indication of exactly where. Another bearing is required, or some other factor that will locate the boat's position on the bearing line, such as a depth reading. Once a satisfactory fix has been plotted it must be enclosed in a circle with a dot to indicate the precise fix position, and the log reading, date and time written alongside.

There are a number of ways in which to plot the boat's position using compass bearings. Some are accurate, some not so accurate – because of the nature of the plot. The main fixes in general use, their accuracy and the procedure for obtaining them are explained on the following pages.

CROSS BEARING FIX

Probably the most accurate and certainly one of the easiest, the cross bearing fix requires bearings of two (preferably three) shore objects taken one after the other, as quickly as possible.

The shore objects should be prominent and identified on the chart with, ideally, an angle of around 30–45° between each. The resulting fix, when bearings are taken of widespread or close-together objects, tends to be less accurate. Too long a time span between taking each bearing will also reduce the accuracy of the fix.

1–2. Take three bearings in fairly quick succession. Convert all three to true bearings, then draw the first bearing on the chart as described earlier for laying off a bearing.

3–4. Repeat with the second and third bearings. Where all three bearings intersect is the fix of the boat's position.

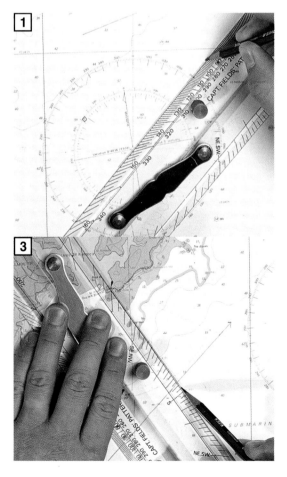

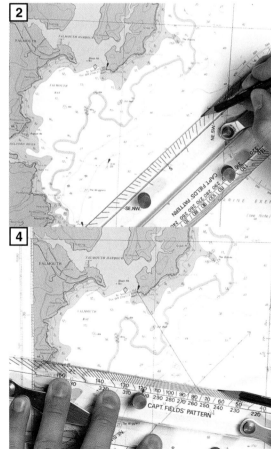

5

5. Place a circle around it to indicate it is an acceptable fix, then note the date, time and log reading beside it on the chart.

COCKED HAT FIX

When conditions are really difficult and the accuracy of the bearings is reduced, they may not intersect exactly but form a triangle. This is known as a 'cocked hat' – see the diagram below. If the cocked hat is fairly small – say half a mile, or a kilometre, across – the centre of the triangle can be accepted as the fix. If the cocked hat is too large, the bearings must be taken again.

If successive attempts fail to reduce the cocked hat to an acceptable size, the intersection of the two bearings closest to the shore is taken as the fix, thus allowing a margin of safety.

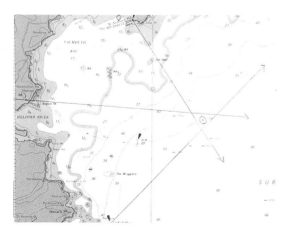

TRANSFERRED BEARING / RUNNING FIX

When only one object is visible, a cross bearing fix is obviously not possible. Here the transferred bearing fix (or running fix, as it is commonly known) is employed, using the hand-bearing compass in conjunction with the distance log. The results are never as accurate as a cross bearing fix, but they do provide reasonable accuracy under most conditions.

- Take a compass bearing of the object and convert it to true.
- At the same time, take the log reading.
- Lay off the bearing on the chart and note the log reading against it.
- Allow the boat to continue along her course line for a period of time, until there has been a reasonable change of bearing – 30° or so.
- Repeat step 1, taking a second bearing of the same object and reading the log. Lay off this second bearing on the chart.
- From the point where the first bearing cuts the course line, measure along the course line the distance run by log between bearings. Mark this point X.
- With the parallel rules, transfer the first bearing along the course line to point X.
- Where the transferred bearing cuts the second bearing is the fix of the boat's position on the second bearing and a circle is placed around it.
- Note the date, time and log reading beside it.
- Repeat the procedure using the second bearing as the first and taking a third bearing and second log reading.

The lesser accuracy of this fix comes about because the two bearings are not taken at the same time. And, in running between the two bearings, tidal streams or currents can interfere with the log reading or push the boat off course. As a general rule, then, one transferred bearing fix is never accepted as being totally accurate. A series of these fixes taken as the boat moves along the track reduces the risk of error, and before long an accurate picture of the boat's progress emerges.

This also applies to other single-bearing fixes, such as Doubling the Angle on the Bow.

Left *The cocked hat fix: because it is often difficult taking accurate compass bearings on a moving boat, cocked hat fixes are common in small boat navigation.*

RUNNING FIX BETWEEN TWO OBJECTS

Where two objects are too far apart for use as cross bearings, the transferred bearing procedure can be used to obtain a running fix.

1–3. When the previously used object has fallen astern sufficiently to create a good angle with the next, take a bearing of the new object and read the log.

4. Measure along the course line the distance run by log from the previous bearing and mark it X.

5–6. Transfer the last bearing of the first object along the course line to point X.

7. Where the transferred first bearing cuts the second bearing is the fix of the boat's position. Circle it and note the time and log reading.

This is a useful fix on long coastlines or where the boat is well offshore and only occasionally are prominent objects available. It is often used at night running between major offshore lighthouses, since no other shore objects are visible. As with the running fix, it is not as accurate as a cross bearing fix, but when a series of these fixes is made, the errors are reduced and the boat's position clearly established.

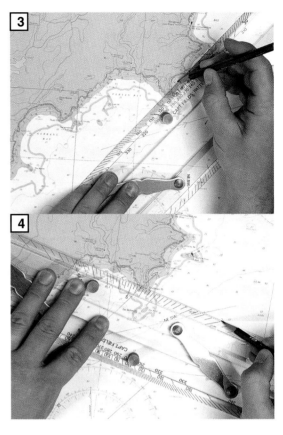

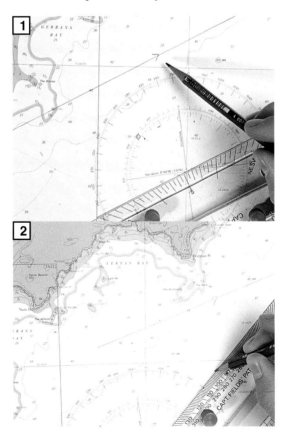

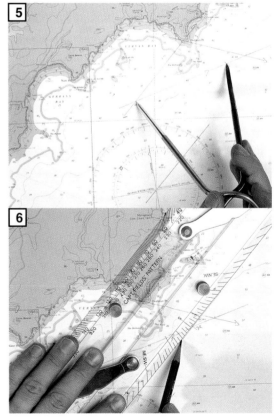

7

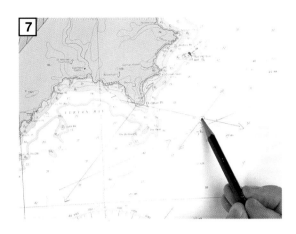

FOUR-POINT BEARING FIX

Not dissimilar to the running fix, this is a handy fix because it does not require the navigator to go below decks. While it can be plotted on the chart like any other fix, it provides a quick check on the boat's progress without leaving the cockpit; a factor that will be appreciated by any crew sleeping below at night. During the day when coasting close inshore, such checks can be done visually and frequently, but at night, with only an occasional light in view, keeping a check on the boat's progress and in particular her distance offshore, is not so easy.

The four-point bearing involved in this fix is the relative bearing that lies four points or 45° on the bow.

- As the boat approaches a light (or shore object), calculate the four-point bearing by subtracting (port bow) or adding (starboard bow) 45° to the course.
- When the light is aligned with this four-point bearing and the boat is on course, read the log.
- Allow the boat to run along the course line until the light is abeam (90°), then read the log again.
- The log distance run between the four-point bearing and the beam bearings is the distance off the shore on the beam bearing. This can be plotted on the chart, or merely used as a visual check of the boat's progress.
- Experienced marine navigators will often determine beforehand some part of the boat's structure that lies on the four-point bearing. In this way, the fix can be carried out without need of the compass by reading the log when the shore object is in line with that part of the boat and reading it again when it is on the beam. The distance run by log between the two bearings is the distance off the shore when abeam. Greater accuracy is obtained if allowance is made for set and drift.

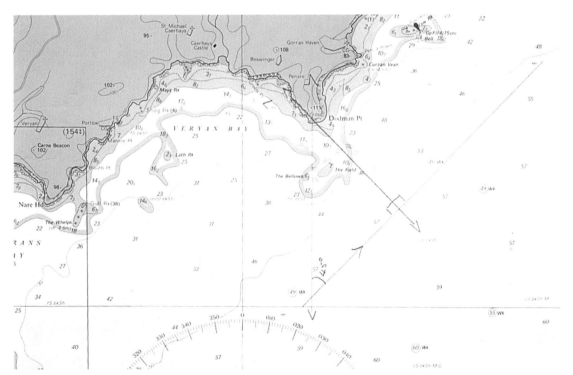

Left *There are eight points of the compass between the bow and the beam of the boat (90°), so the four-point bearing is at 45° to the bow. The four-point bearing and the beam bearing together with the course line create an isosceles triangle.*

DOUBLING THE ANGLE ON THE BOW FIX

An adaptation of the four-point bearing fix (the beam bearing is double the four-point bearing), this fix follows the same procedure:

- Take a bearing at any point when the object is fairly fine on the bow.
- Read the log.
- Calculate the relative bearing between the course line and the bearing.
- Allow the boat to run on until the relative bearing has doubled.
- Read the log again.

- The distance run by log between the two relative bearings is the distance off the object on the second bearing. Plot it on the chart.
- Continue on course until the second relative bearing has doubled. Read the log again.
- The distance run by log between second and third bearings is the distance off the object on the third bearing. Plot it on the chart.

This routine will provide a series of fixes that, like the running fix, will indicate the boat's progress as it moves past the object.

This fix works on the principle of an isosceles triangle: equal angles, equal sides.

Right *Doubling the angle on the bow fix: because only two bearings are used, a single fix cannot be relied on, thus a series of fixes is made to establish the boat's position and progress.*

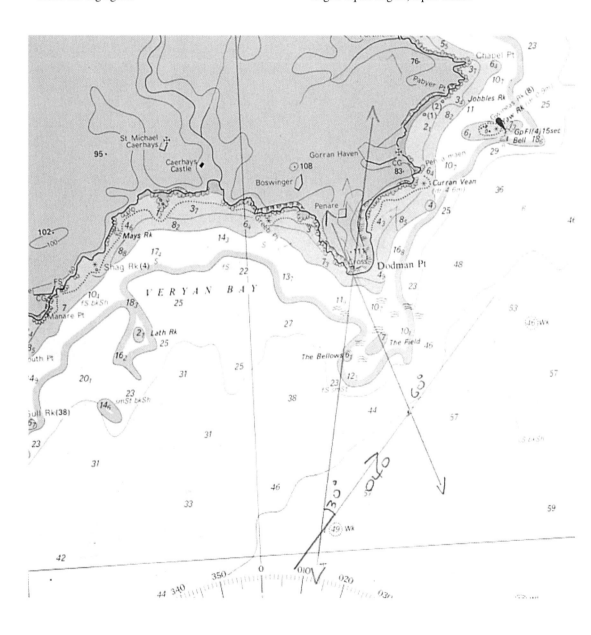

FIX BY VERTICAL SEXTANT ANGLE

This can be one of the most accurate forms of fixing the boat's position, but it involves the use of a sextant – not carried by many yachts on coastal passages – and requires the boat to be fairly close to the shore. However, a sextant is vital for vessels making a close inshore run, as it is a precision instrument and gives very accurate results. A set of nautical tables may also be required:

• On the chart, select a high object on the coastline and note the height listed beside it. Lighthouses are ideal for this.

• Sight up the lighthouse in the sextant and bring the centre of the light to sea level in the telescope.

• Read off the angle measured by the sextant.

• Take a compass bearing of the light, convert it to true and lay it off on the chart.

• In any nautical tables enter the Distance by Sextant Angle table and read off the distance with the height of the light as one argument and the sextant reading the other. This can also be done using a simple right-angle triangle calculation, the distance off being the base of the triangle.

• Measure the distance found along the compass bearing to provide an accurate fix of the boat's position on the chart.

Left *A high shore object, such as a cliff, a lighthouse or a building, that is well marked on the chart can be used for sextant angle fixes. The height is taken from the chart.*

Left *Fix by vertical sextant angle: the bearing is laid off on the chart and the distance found by sextant angle is marked along it for a very accurate close inshore fix.*

Below *The best sextant angle fixes are with objects close to the shoreline.*

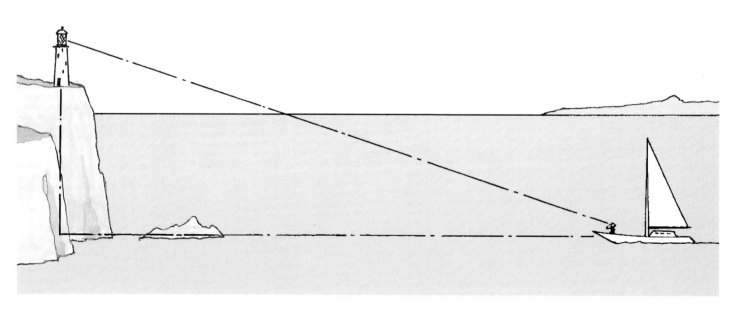

Right *When navigating well off-shore or crossing long stretches of open water (and in particular when making a landfall after an ocean crossing), the extreme range fix is often the only means of establishing the boat's position.*

EXTREME RANGE FIX

Long-range lights located along the coastline can often be seen by the 'loom' of their beams sweeping across the sky like searchlights, long before the light itself appears. When the light does appear, it 'breaks' suddenly over the horizon and the loom is replaced by a brilliant flash. This moment of the light breaking over the horizon offers the opportunity to obtain a good fix of the vessel's position. It is particularly useful when making a landfall after a passage over open sea, as it allows the navigator to adjust course while still well away from the land.

The only requirements are a clear night, a powerful light and a volume of nautical tables. The 'height of eye' used in the tables is the height of the observer's eye above sea level.

- Watch the loom of the light and then identify it from the chart.
- At the moment the light breaks, take a bearing and lay it off on the chart.
- In any volume of nautical tables enter the Extreme Range table with the height of eye of the observer and the height of the lighthouse taken from the chart. Take out the extreme range of the light.
- Measure this distance along the bearing on the chart to obtain a good fix of the boat's position.

Below *Plotting an extreme range fix.*

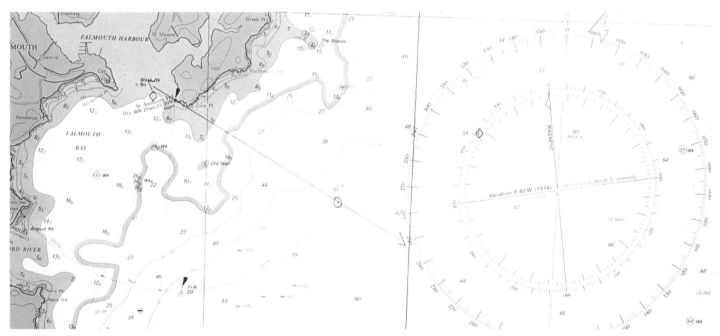

COUNTERING AN UNKNOWN SET

Known factors that are likely to push the boat off course, such as leeway, known currents and tidal streams, can be applied to the course beforehand to counter their effect and hold the boat on course.

Despite such corrections, though, the boat will almost certainly still be pushed off course by other, unknown factors.

Close to a coast, for example, tidal streams can do all sorts of strange things, and it is not unknown for back eddies or rips sweeping out of bays to actually reverse the predicted flow. Leeway can be difficult to ascertain accurately because it varies in different wind strengths and as the boat heels. Even bad steering can be part of this unknown factor.

Whatever the cause, the effect is to push the boat off course by an unpredictable amount. In order to counter this, the set must first be measured. Then, when it has been determined, it is applied to the course to counter any future effect.

An unknown set is countered as follows:

- As the boat progresses, take a series of fixes over, say, two or three hours, and plot them on the chart.
- From the first fix, draw a line through the subsequent fixes to the last fix and measure it on the compass rose. This is known as the Course Made Good (CMG).
- The difference between the course steered and the CMG is the unknown set affecting the vessel, measured in degrees.
- From the last fix position draw a line to the arrival position or next alter-course position and measure it on the compass rose.
- To this new course apply compass error, leeway and known set, as before. Then apply the newly found (unknown) set in the opposite direction to which it has been affecting the boat. This will provide the course to steer to destination, allowing for all factors including the unknown set. Since the unknown set is created by varying factors, the procedure must be repeated at regular intervals.

Below *Countering an unknown set: unknown factors that push the boat off course cannot be counteracted until their effect is known. The difference between the course steered and the course made good over a period of time is the amount the boat is being set off course. When this has been found, it is then applied in order to achieve the required course.*

CELESTIAL NAVIGATION

Until the recent advent of electronic systems, once out of sight of land navigators had nothing but celestial objects with which to find their way around the oceans of the world.

While this may appear to the uninitiated to be a complex and difficult task, in fact it is relatively simple, particularly with today's modern navigational aids. Even the traditional methods using the sextant are relatively easy, while radio time signals and modern sight reduction tables take much of the drudgery out of the earlier mathematical formulae and calculations.

THE EQUIPMENT

Although most of the equipment required for navigation by sun, moon, planets and stars need not be expensive, the sextant is the key instrument and it would be false economy to save money on this item.

The quality of the better brands always pays dividends in terms of simplicity, ease of use and accuracy, all of which are important when trying to take celestial sights in difficult sea conditions. The chronometer, once a very expensive item, is mostly replaced these days by a reliable watch checked daily by radio time signals.

Other than the sextant and chronometer, the equipment required for traditional navigation on an ocean passage is relatively inexpensive, but should certainly include the items listed overleaf.

Opposite *A steady hand and a steady eye are necessary for accurate sextant sights.*

- Charts (small-scale for ocean crossing, large-scale for landfall and coasting; current charts)
- Chart instruments
- Short-wave radio (for time signals)
- Nautical Almanac
- Sight reduction tables (with information for resolving sextant sights)
- Nautical tables
- Star plotter (a gadget to help novice navigators identify stars)
- Plotting sheets
- List of Radio Navigation Aids (for time signals, Loran – a form of electronic navigation, etc.)
- Pilots (volumes containing detailed information on coastlines, land fall or ocean hazards)
- Other relevant publications, depending on the passage and intended destination.

Right top *Venus, the closest planet to earth, is the brightest and most useful for celestial sights. Some of the other planets can also be used, if they are bright enough and in the right position.*

Right bottom *The phases of the moon are created by the relative position of the sun. In the diagram the sun would be located out of frame to the right.*

Below *Identifying stars by their constellation is a good way to go about selecting stars for sight taking. Orion has a number of useful stars, of which Rigel and Betelgeuse are the brightest. Orion's Belt leads to Sirius and Aldebaran.*

THE HEAVENLY BODIES

A quick glance at the night sky indicates that there are perhaps trillions of heavenly bodies for the navigator to choose from. Most of the stars are unsuitable for navigation, though, because they are too small, not bright enough or not conveniently placed. The main navigational stars are listed in the Nautical Almanac, along with the sun, moon and planets. It is from this group that the navigator selects those most suitable for sight taking. The sun is obviously of use only during daylight hours, but at night there is the full range of selected stars, the planets and the moon.

STARS

Stars are a part of earth's galaxy (the Milky Way) but not part of its solar system. The stars selected for sight taking are usually very bright and well spaced across the heavens. As with coastal navigation, where the bearings of shore objects are preferably spaced about 30–45° apart, so with celestial navigation. Stars that are diametrically opposite another or too close together do not produce accurate results.

When selecting three or four stars for a dawn or dusk sight it is important to identify them quickly, because the period when the stars and a clear-cut horizon are visible at the same time is fairly short. Initially it might be necessary to use a starfinder chart, but after a day or two of sight taking, the position of each star will be known from its location at the previous day's sights.

The position of the planets

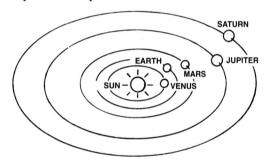

The phases of the moon

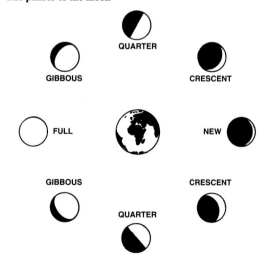

THE NAUTICAL ALMANAC

There are a number of Nautical Almanacs available; official volumes published by the Hydrographic Department of the respective navies around the world, and privately published almanacs, some of which are preferred by experienced navigators.

Almanacs are produced every year, and contain the positions of all heavenly bodies used for navigation for every second of every day of the whole year. The declination (often shortened to 'dec') and the GHA (Greenwich Hour Angle, see page 76) are listed for sun, moon and planets while the stars are listed as Aries and SHA (Sidereal Hour Angle, see page 77). The main pages are listed for each hour of GMT while a table of increments and corrections allows interpolations for minutes and seconds.

Other information, such as sunrise and sunset, moonrise and moonset times and twilights are also carried on the main pages, while other tables, such as the Pole Star Tables and information of use in navigation, including star charts, are carried at the back. Sight Reduction Tables and information on using calculators and computers for resolving sight computations are also provided in some almanacs.

PLANETS

Planets are a part of earth's solar system and therefore revolve around the sun. Of the nine planets, only four are used for navigation: Venus, Mars, Jupiter and Saturn (the others are not bright enough to give a positive reading in the sextant). Venus is the most popular of these because it is the brightest – so much so that it can sometimes be seen during the day.

The movements of navigational planets across the sky are tabulated daily in the Nautical Almanac.

A planet is easily distinguished from a star because it has a steady light and does not twinkle.

THE MOON

Because of its size and brilliance, the moon can often be seen during the day as well as at night; it therefore makes a useful partner to the sun for crossed LOP (Line of Position) sights. However, the moon is a troublesome body, as its orbit sometimes makes it unavailable at times. In addition, it can sometimes hang at an awkward angle in the sky, making it difficult to place correctly on the horizon when taking a sextant sight. The computation of a moon sight is more involved than those for the sun or planets. This puts it out of favour with quite a few navigators.

THE SUN

For sights and calculations, the sun is the navigator's favourite celestial body. It is big and clearly visible, often through light layers of cloud, for most of the day. Most sight calculations are simpler using the sun than those involving other heavenly bodies, and although there are times of the day when sun sights are best taken, there is no reason why they cannot be taken at any time.

Apart from its use for position fixing, the sun is also useful for other aspects of navigation: at noon it is the boat's timekeeper, for it provides a means of checking the clocks on board; at dawn and dusk it can be used to check the boat's compasses.

Although it seems to follow a steady path across the sky from east to west each day, the sun is also moving slowly north and south.

In the course of a year it moves from the Tropic of Cancer (23½° North latitude) to the Tropic of Capricorn (23½° South latitude) and back, creating the seasons in both hemispheres. This movement must be taken into consideration when using the sun for navigation, and for this reason, the position of the sun (in celestial latitude and longitude) is tabulated in the Nautical Almanac for every second of every day of every year.

Above *Obtaining a clear horizon for sight taking may mean scrambling around the boat to find a suitable position. Mast, sails and rigging can make the navigator's task difficult.*

DETERMINING LHA OF SIRIUS USING HOUR ANGLE DIAGRAM

Example: To find the LHA of Sirius:

The LHA = GHA + or - Long = OX.

GHA = GHA Aries + SHA i.e. GX = GR + RX.

Longitude is GO. Therefore: OX = GR + RX - GO.

LHA = GHA Aries + SHA - Long.

There are many combinations that will need to be worked out, depending on the heavenly body being used, its location, its relation to the boat and the position of other factors such as Aries and longitude.

By using the diagram even inexperienced navigators should be able to resolve such problems quite easily.

Right Noon on board the vessel (12:00 Local Mean Time, or LMT – see page 87) is when the sun crosses the meridian. To find GMT of noon on board, apply the longitude.

TIME AND LONGITUDE

The standard time adopted for navigation anywhere is what's known as Universal Time (UT) (formerly Greenwich Mean Time, although both terms are still in common use). Standard time is sometimes known as 'Zulu', as the world is divided into time zones that are given alphabetical letters, and Greenwich lies in the 'Z' zone.

The sun crosses the Greenwich meridian at noon each day, on its 24-hour (360°) journey around the world. Longitude also begins at Greenwich and travels 360° around the world, hence the relationship between time and longitude.

After crossing the Greenwich meridian at noon GMT (12:00), the sun moves westward covering 15° of longitude every hour. Thus at any point during its westward travels, the GMT is equal to the sun's GHA (converted to time) + 12:00 hours (the time the sun crossed the Greenwich meridian).

As indicated in an example of the hour angle diagram below, when the sun crosses the meridian on which a vessel is located, the GMT of that meridian passage equals the westerly longitude of the vessel (with the conversion to time and the addition of 12 hours). Similarly, the westerly longitude of the vessel is obviously the same as the sun's GHA at that time.

A practical application of this situation is when taking the noon sight at sea – latitude by meridian altitude. It is vital that this sight is taken at precisely the moment the sun crosses the meridian. Although this exact moment will be determined by the movement of the sun in the telescope, the navigator will need to have some indication of when to take out the sextant and prepare for the meridian passage.

If the boat's noon Dead Reckoning (DR) longitude is converted into time and 12 hours are added, the approximate GMT of meridian passage will be obtained. If the boat is in longitude 120° West, for example, the sun will take eight hours to travel from the Greenwich meridian to the boat's meridian. Since it crosses the Greenwich meridian at 12:00 GMT, the time of meridian passage at the boat will be eight hours later, i.e. 20:00 GMT.

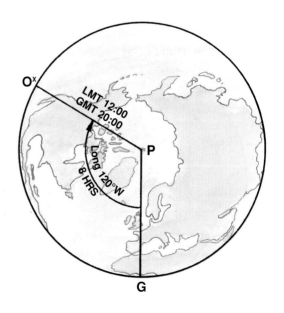

SIGHT TAKING

It is important that before each sight the sextant is checked for instrument errors by using the horizon or a star (see pages 29–33). When the sextant reading is taken, the corrections can be applied to ensure accurate readings.

When a sight is to be taken, the sun is brought down in the sextant telescope until it is on the horizon, then the sextant is rocked to ensure that the instrument is absolutely vertical at the time of taking the reading. This is not easy, because the movement of the boat makes it hard to hold the sun exactly on the horizon, as does the natural tendency of any boat to yaw (swing from side to side) on either side of the course line. If conditions are bad it may be necessary to take a quick series of sights to obtain an average reading, after discarding obviously erroneous sights, and reduce the likelihood of errors. The procedure is the same with planets and stars.

As well as accurate sight taking, exact timing is also vital – so much so that a wise navigator will employ one of the crew to take the time, since errors can creep in if one person tries to juggle the sextant and chronometer. The usual practice is for the navigator to brace into the rigging or against the cabin as he or she goes through the sight-taking routine. At the instant the navigator feels the reading is accurate, the person with the watch will be asked to take the GMT

The
Computations

There are a number of methods of resolving celestial sights. Some navigators enjoy using the traditional methods while others prefer the relative simplicity and accuracy of computers and calculators. While the electronic methods are certainly easier, it would be an unwise yacht owner who set off across an ocean relying solely on these methods to handle celestial navigation.

When the computer crashes, the calculator is dropped or the batteries run out, the ocean is a big place in which to be stranded with no means of working out sights.

THE SIGHT FORM

Navigators with a high level of mathematical expertise may use involved trigonometrical formulae, such as the Marc St Hilaire method, to resolve their sights, but under the less than ideal conditions of a small boat in a seaway, the average person will be only too happy to accept any system which will make sight computations easier. Marc St Hilaire was a French navigator who developed a convenient method of working out sextant sights by employing spherical trigonometry; this method was widely used until the Sight Reduction Method replaced it.

Modern methods have simplified the mathematics, and books and forms have been devised to make sight working very much simpler.

A method favoured by most mariners is known as 'sight reduction', which simplifies the sight computation to the point

Opposite You can't get away with only electronic methods of navigation... Without a knowledge of the celestial navigation calculations, you may find yourself lost at sea.

Below *A stable platform and a clear horizon are essential for accurate sight taking. Dusk and dawn are ideal times, as the stars are still visible and the horizon is well defined.*

where it amounts to little more than filling in a form and adding up a few lines of figures.

The terms used on this sight form may seem a little daunting, but they are not as complex as they appear, and most are effectively just a code or name; some, such as GHA, SHA and dec, are already familiar. The other main terms used are as follows:

Chosen lat and long

Because the main pages of the Sight Reduction tables are in whole degrees, all values for use in these tables must be also reduced to degrees, even DR lat, which is then renamed 'chosen lat'. These adjustments are known as 'tab' (tabulated) values. In the case of latitude this simply means taking the DR lat to the nearest whole degree. The chosen long is a little more complex and is best explained by the example given on page 88 in a worked sight.

Ho

This is the term used for the true or observed altitude (H for altitude, o for observed), taken from the sextant and corrected for sextant errors.

Hc

This is the calculated altitude (c for computed or calculated), which is derived by calculation from the assumed position of the boat chosen lat/long.

Since Hc is based on an estimated altitude and Ho is the observed (true) altitude, broadly speaking the difference between Hc and Ho is the difference between where the boat is thought to be and where the observations indicate it really is!

Int

The difference between Hc and Ho is called the intercept.

d

This is what might be termed a 'stepping stone' between the main pages and the interpolation tables and represents the altitude difference. Once d has been used in the tables, it is discarded.

Z

'Z' is the azimuth angle or bearing of the heavenly body measured eastward or westward through 180° from north or south.

ZX

'ZX' is the zenith distance that is found by subtracting Ho from 90°.

Zn

'Zn' is the true bearing of the body. In north latitude, if LHA is greater than 180°, Zn = Z. If LHA is less than 180°, Zn = 360 - Z.

In south latitude, if the LHA is greater than 180°, Zn = 180° - Z. If the LHA is less than 180°, Zn = 180° + Z. The result is the true bearing of the body and is used to plot the fix on the chart.

Dip

The dip of the sea horizon, called simply dip, is the correction to the sextant altitude for the curve of the sea horizon. It is found in the Nautical Almanac and is always subtracted.

Altitude correction

This is a single correction for a number of small but significant errors that affect the sextant altitude. It is found in the Nautical Almanac.

One such error is refraction, which is the result of the sun's rays being bent as they enter earth's atmosphere, which makes the sun appear in an incorrect position. A similar effect causes a stick in a bucket of water to appear bent.

Altitude correction is also sometimes known as Main correction.

LMT

This means local mean time, or time kept on board the boat. Because the boat is moving across the face of the globe, LMT must be constantly adjusted, usually once a day, according to the change in longitude. For this reason LMT is used for shipboard activities, Universal Time/GMT is used for navigation.

Top left *Dip is the result of landing the sun (in the sextant) on the false horizon created by the curvature of the earth (point A). The true horizon level is at B. The correction for the curve is the dip.*

Bottom left *Deflection of the sun's image through atmospheric refractions is one factor in the correction of altitude.*

Left *Altitude Correction tables found in the Nautical Almanac.*

Below *The dip table is usually on the inside cover of the Nautical Almanac.*

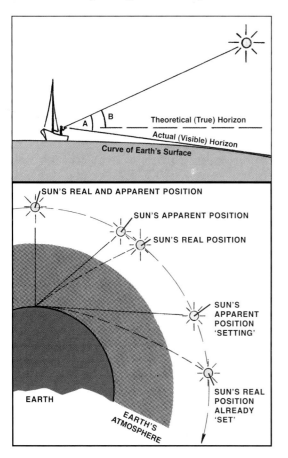

OCT–MAR	SUN	APR–SEPT		STARS AND PLANETS	
App. Alt.	Lower Upper Limb Limb	App. Alt.	Lower Upper Limb Limb	App. Alt. Corr	App. Additional Alt. Corr
° ′		° ′		° ′	1985
9 34	+ 10·8 – 21 5	9 36	+ 10·6 – 21.2	9 56 – 5.3	VENUS
9 45	+ 10·9 – 21 4	9 51	+ 10.7 – 21.1	10 08 – 5.2	Jan 1 – Feb 4
9 56	+ 11·0 – 21 3	10 03	+ 10.8 – 21.0	10 20 – 5.1	° ′
10 08	+ 11·1 – 21 2	10 15	+ 10.9 – 20.9	10 33 – 5.0	0 + 0.2
10 21	+ 11·2 – 21 1	10 27	+ 11.0 – 20.8	10 46 – 4.9	41 + 0.1
10 34	+ 11·3 – 21 0	10 40	+ 11.1 – 20.7	11 00 – 4.8	76
10 47	+ 11·4 – 20 9	10 54	+ 11.2 – 20.6	11 14 – 4.7	Feb 5 – Feb 28
11 01	+ 11·5 – 20 8	11 08	+ 11.3 – 20.5	11 29 – 4.6	° ′
11 15	+ 11·6 – 20 7	11 23	+ 11.4 – 20.4	11 45 – 4.5	0 + 0.3
11 30	+ 11·7 – 20 6	11 38	+ 11.5 – 20.3	12 01 – 4.4	34 + 0.2
11 46	+ 11·8 – 20 5	11 54	+ 11.6 – 20.2	12 18 – 4.3	60 + 0.1
12 02	+ 11·9 – 20 4	12 10	+ 11.7 – 20.1	12 35 – 4.2	80
12 19	+ 12·0 – 20 3	12 28	+ 11.8 – 20.0	12 54 – 4.2	Mar 1 – Mar 16
12 37	+ 12·1 – 20 2	12 46	+ 11.9 – 19.9	13 13 – 4.1	° ′
12 55	+ 12·2 – 20 1	13 05	+ 12.0 – 19.8	13 33 – 3.9	0 + 0.4
13 14	+ 12·3 – 20 0	13 24	+ 12.1 – 19.7	13 54 – 3.8	29 + 0.3
13 35	+ 12·4 – 19 9	13 45	+ 12.2 – 19.6	14 16 – 3.7	51 + 0.2
13 56	+ 12·5 – 19 8	14 07	+ 12.3 – 19.5	14 40 – 3.6	68 + 0.1
14 18	+ 12·6 – 19 7	14 30	+ 12.4 – 19.4	15 04 – 3.5	83
14 42	+ 12·7 – 19 6	14 54	+ 12.5 – 19.3	15 30 – 3.4	Mar 17 – Apr 21
15 06	+ 12·8 – 19 5	15 19	+ 12.6 – 19.2	15 57 – 3.3	° ′
15 32	+ 12·9 – 19 4	15 46	+ 12.7 – 19.1	16 26 – 3.2	0 + 0.5
15 59	+ 13·0 – 19 3	16 14	+ 12.8 – 19.0	16 56 – 3.1	26 + 0.4
16 28	+ 13·1 – 19 2	16 44	+ 12.9 – 18.9	17 28 – 3.0	46 + 0.3
16 59	+ 13·2 – 19 1	17 15	+ 13.0 – 18.8	18 02 – 2.9	60 + 0.2
17 32	+ 13·3 – 19 0	17 48	+ 13.1 – 18.7	18 38 – 2.8	73 + 0.1
18 06	+ 13·4 – 18 9	18 24	+ 13.2 – 18.6	19 17 – 2.7	84
18 42	+ 13·5 – 18 8	19 01	+ 13.3 – 18.5	19 58 – 2.6	Apr 22 – May 7
19 21	+ 13·6 – 18 7	19 42	+ 13.4 – 18.4	20 42 – 2.5	° ′
20 03	+ 13·7 – 18 6	20 25	+ 13.5 – 18.3	21 28 – 2.4	0 + 0.4
20 48	+ 13·8 – 18 5	21 11	+ 13.6 – 18.2	22 19 – 2.3	29 + 0.3
21 35	+ 13·9 – 18 4	22 00	+ 13.7 – 18.1	23 13 – 2.2	51 + 0.2
22 26	+ 14·0 – 18 3	22 54	+ 13.8 – 18.0	24 11 – 2.1	68 + 0.1
23 22	+ 14·1 – 18 2	23 51	+ 13.9 – 17.9	25 14 – 2.0	83
24 21	+ 14·2 – 18 1	24 53	+ 14.0 – 17.8	26 22 – 1.9	May 8 – May 29
25 26	+ 14·3 – 18 0	26 00	+ 14.1 – 17.7	27 36 – 1.8	° ′
26 36	+ 14·4 – 17 9	27 13	+ 14.2 – 17.6	28 56 – 1.7	0 + 0.3
27 52	+ 14·5 – 17 8	28 33	+ 14.3 – 17.5	30 24 – 1.6	34 + 0.2
29 15	+ 14·6 – 17 7	30 00	+ 14.4 – 17.4	32 00 – 1.5	60 + 0.1
30 46	+ 14·7 – 17 6	31 35	+ 14.5 – 17.3	33 45 – 1.4	80
32 26	+ 14·8 – 17 5	33 20	+ 14.6 – 17.2	35 40 – 1.3	May 30 – July 18
34 17	+ 14·9 – 17 4	35 17	+ 14.7 – 17.1	37 48 – 1.2	° ′
					0 + 0.2
					41 + 0.1
					76
					July 14 – Dec 31
					° ′
					0 + 0.2
					60
					MARS
					Jan 1 – Dec 31
					° ′
					0 + 0.1
					60

DIP					
Ht of Eye	Corr	Ht of Eye	Ht of Eye	Corr	
m ′		ft	m ′		
2·4		8·0	1·0 – 1 8		
2·6 – 2·8		8·6	1·5 – 2 2		
2·8 – 2·9		9·2	2·0 – 2 5		
3·0 – 3·0		9·8	2·5 – 2 8		
3·2 – 3·1		10·5	3·0 – 3 0		
3·4 – 3·2		11·2	**See Table**		
3·6 – 3·3		11·9	←		
3·8 – 3·4		12·6	m ′		
4·0 – 3·5		13·3	20 – 7 9		
4·3 – 3·6		14·1	22 – 8 3		
4·5 – 3·7		14·9	24 – 8 6		
4·7 – 3·8		15·7	26 – 9.0		
5·0 – 3·9		16·5	28 – 9 3		
5·2 – 4·0		17·4			
5·5 – 4·1		18·3	30 – 9 3		
5·8 – 4·2		19·1	32 – 9 6		
6·1 – 4·3		20·1	34 – 10 0		
6·3 – 4·4		21·0	36 – 10 3		
6·6 – 4·5		22·0	38 – 10 6		
6·9 – 4·6		22·9			
7·2 – 4·7		23·9	40 – 11.1		
7·5 – 4·8		24·9	42 – 11 4		
7·9 – 4·9		26·0	44 – 11 7		
8·2 – 5·0		27·1	46 – 11 9		
8·5 – 5·1		28·1	48 – 12 2		
8·8 – 5·2		29·2	ft.		
9·2 – 5·3		30·4	2 – 1 4		
9·5 – 5·4		31·5	4 – 1 9		
9·9 – 5·5		32·7	6 – 2 4		
10·3 – 5·7		33·9	8 – 2.7		
10·6 – 5·8		35·1	10 – 3.1		

Section II

The sextant reading (36°05') is taken from the instrument and entered at the top of this section, then corrected as follows:

- Apply the index error (-1.0') to obtain the obs alt (36°04').
- Apply the dip (-3.0') using a height of eye of 3 metres to obtain the app alt (36°01').
- Apply the altitude correction from the Nautical Almanac for the October–March column (+14.9') to obtain the true alt or Ho (36°15.9').

Section III

For this section, the Nautical Almanac is entered on the relevant date (15 December 2001).

- Using GMT (05h), take out the GHA from the sun column (256°4.3') and enter it on the form.
- From the Increments and Corrections table at the back of the Almanac, take out the increment for 54 mins and 8 secs and enter it on the form (13°32').
- Add these two to obtain the total GHA for the GMT of sight (269°46.3').
- The tab LHA is required and this is found by adding east longitude to or subtracting west longitude from the GHA. In order to eliminate the minutes, the nearest longitude is chosen which will, when applied to the GHA, result in whole degrees. In this case, because GHA is to be added to the longitude, a chosen longitude of 151°13.7' will be necessary, giving a tab LHA of 61°.
- From the Nautical Almanac Daily Pages, obtain the sun's declination at the GMT of sight. A little interpolation might be needed here. Enter the degrees of dec (23°S) as tab dec, and the minutes (16°.2') as dec inc, on the form.
- Enter the chosen latitude (DR lat to the nearest degree) on the last line of this section (35°S).

Section IV

Now the Sight Reduction tables come into play (NP401 is used in this example):

- Turn to to the double page headed LHA 61°. Since dec and lat are both named south, the left-hand pages will be used.

- In the column headed 35 (chosen lat), and against the tab dec (23) in the side column, take out the three factors Hc (36°08.0'), d (+27.4'), Z (85.4°) and enter them in their respective positions on the sight form.
- At the top or the bottom of the double page, small print indicates the application of Z to find Zn. In this case, since the boat is in south latitudes and the LHA is less than 180, then Zn = 180 + Z, i.e. Zn = 265.4°).
- From the Interpolation tables on the inside cover of the Sight Reduction tables, take out the altitude correction factors.
- With the dec inc (16.2') down the side and the tens of 'd' in the main table (20), take out the first correction to Hc (5.4') and enter it on the form where indicated.
- There are 7.4 remaining minutes of 'd'. In the Sight Reduction table, follow the units column (7') down the right-hand table to the block which covers the dec inc (16.0' to 17.0'). In the 7' column, against the decimal 0.4 will be found the second correction to Hc (2.0').

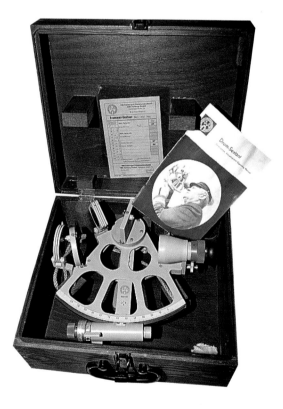

Right As it is the mainstay of celestial navigation – and is often used for coastal navigation – the sextant with its mirrors and glass is treated with great care by navigators.

- Add the two corrections to find the total correction (7.3) and then apply this to the Hc as indicated by 'd' (in this case +). The result is the corrected Hc (36°15.3').

- The difference between Ho and Hc (0.6') is the Intercept and is named TOWARDS (the sun) if Ho is greater than Hc, or AWAY, if the reverse is the case. Here it will be towards. The sight computation is now complete and ready to plot on the chart.

SIGHT REDUCTION USING THE PLANETS

While the shooting of a planet sight with a sextant is more difficult than with the sun, the computations using the sight reduction method are almost identical. However, they have two additional factors: 'v' and 'd' corrections.

These are very small corrections and are taken from the bottom of the page in the Nautical Almanac Daily Pages: v applies to the GHA and d to the declination as indicated.

SIGHT REDUCTION USING THE STARS

Again, the main difficulty with star sights is obtaining an accurate sextant reading, for stars are always mere pinpoints of light in the sextant and the navigator needs a great deal of practice before he or she is able to land them on the horizon properly.

Add to this the fact that the horizon will be only half lighted while the navigator is attempting the sight – since star sights are taken at dawn and dusk – and the problems are compounded.

As far as the sight reduction computation is concerned, it varies only a little from that used with sun and planets. The main difference lies in obtaining the GHA, as with stars this value is not listed on a daily basis in the Nautical Almanac.

This GHA is compiled by taking the GHA of Aries for the GMT of the sight from the Daily Pages and adding it to the star's SHA, found on a separate page of the Almanac. Once this angle is obtained, the navigator will continue the sight reduction as for the sun and planets.

SIGHT REDUCTION USING THE MOON

Most small-boat navigators avoid using the moon for sights – it can be difficult to shoot in the sextant, particularly if it is upside down or at an awkward angle where the lower limb cannot be used.

The upper limb can be used, but this again, is difficult to land on the horizon since the 'rocking' of the sextant creates an inverted swing and a correction must also be made to the sight calculations. This, plus the fact that the moon has a cycle of 29.5 days, makes moon sight computations more complex than those for sun, stars and planets.

Below Sight Reduction Form for Line of Position (LOP) workings.

SIGHT REDUCTION FORM

SECTION 1

BODY: Sun   DATE: 15 December 2001   LMT: 16:00 hrs

GMT: 05h 54m 08s   DR Lat: 35° 17' S   DR Long: 151° 01' E

SECTION 2

Sextant Alt	36° 05.0'
Index Error	01.0' -
Obs Alt	36° 04.0'
Dip	03.0' -
App Alt	36° 01.0' -
Alt Corr	14.9' +
True Alt (Ho)	

SECTION 3

GHA	256° 14.3'
Inc	13° 32.0' +
SHA	(stars)
Total GHA	269° 46.3'
Chosen Long	151° 13.7'
Tab LHA	61°
Tab Dec	23°
Dec Inc	16.2'
Chosen Lat	35° S

SECTION 4

TABLES:

	Hc 36° 08.0'	d +27.4'	Z 85.4°	
Corr (i)	5.3'			180.0° +
Corr (ii)	2.0'			
Total corr	7.3'		Zn	265.4°
Hc	36° 15.3'			
Ho	36° 15.9'			
INT	0.5' TOWARDS			

- Locate the chosen lat and chosen long of the first star on the plotting sheet.
- With the parallel rules and the compass rose, lay off the azimuth (Zn) through this position in the direction of the star and also in the opposite direction.
- Using the latitude scale on the plotting sheet, measure the intercept from the chosen position towards or away from the star, as indicated.
- Through this point draw a line at right angles to the azimuth. This is the LOP and the boat's position must lie somewhere along it.
- Lay off the remaining three stars in the same way, ensuring that each azimuth is drawn from its own chosen long.
- Where all LOPs intersect (most likely with a cocked hat) is the boat's position and the latitude and longitude can be taken off and transferred to the working chart.

TRANSFERRED LOPS

When only a single sight is taken, as with the sun in morning and afternoon sights, the plotting is done in exactly the same way, but only a single LOP will result, not a full fix. However, in just the same way that a bearing is transferred along the course line to give a running fix in coastal navigation, so a celestial LOP can be transferred along the course line to cross with another at some later time.

In the case of the morning sun sight, its LOP is plotted and then run up the course line for the log distance to cross with the noon latitude, which can then be run on and crossed with a second LOP taken later in the afternoon. This is part of the procedure described earlier, under the title 'the day's work' on page 80, which provides a LOP in the morning, a transferred fix position at noon and another LOP in the afternoon.

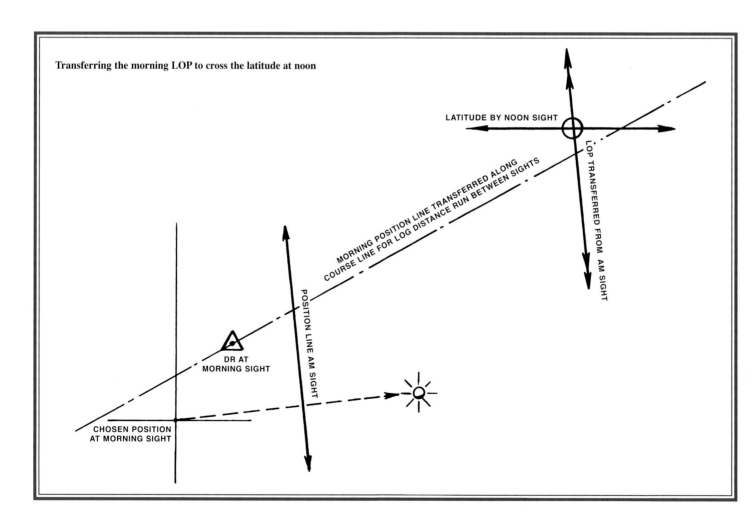

Transferring the morning LOP to cross the latitude at noon

LATITUDE BY NOON SIGHT

LOP TRANSFERRED FROM AM SIGHT

MORNING POSITION LINE TRANSFERRED ALONG COURSE LINE FOR LOG DISTANCE RUN BETWEEN SIGHTS

POSITION LINE AM SIGHT

DR AT MORNING SIGHT

CHOSEN POSITION AT MORNING SIGHT

CHECKING THE COMPASS AT SEA

Many things can happen to a magnetic compass during an ocean passage: a needle may drop off, or stray magnetic influences may crop up, and these may not always be obvious. Electronic compasses, too, can be subject to errors that, unless there is some means of detecting the problem, can seriously affect the boat's navigation.

A simple routine undertaken each morning or evening enables the compass to be checked regularly and accurately each day. The method is referred to as an 'amplitude', and it involves taking a bearing of the sun as it rises above or sinks onto the horizon at the start or finish of the day. An amplitude is the number of degrees north or south of due east (morning) or west (afternoon) that the sun rises or sets.

Do the following:

- As the sun touches the horizon with its lower edge, rising or falling, take a bearing with the compass and at the same time note the GMT. Apply compass error to convert the compass bearing to true.
- From the Nautical Almanac, take out the sun's declination for the GMT.
- Go to the amplitude table, found in most volumes of nautical tables, and with the arguments declination and DR latitude, take out the amplitude.
- By comparing the true bearing of the amplitude with the true bearing taken on the compass, any error in the compass will be revealed.

Above *When checking the compass at sea, it is best to do so at sunrise or sunset.*

Left *An azimuth can be obtained at any time of day, but the amplitude is considered to be more accurate as the sun is low on the horizon, allowing a more accurate compass bearing to be taken.*

Far left *Most ocean-going yachts carry computers to assist with navigation computations as well as provide useful information about currents and weather.*

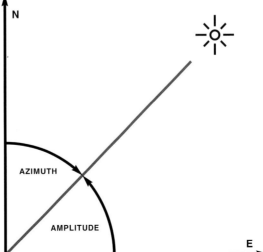

CROSSING THE OCEANS

Over 70 per cent of the earth's surface is covered with salt water, and that water is constantly on the move – not just as a result of the earth's rotation, but also because of widely varying factors such as the effect of winds, continental contours and, of course, the gravitational influence of the moon.

The air around the world is also constantly moving, again under the influence of earth's rotation and due to global and local factors. Small wonder, then, that the ocean navigator, heading out into an untamed and mostly unpredictable environment, will feel some apprehension at what lies ahead. Survival and safe arrival will to a large extent depend on how carefully the passage has been planned and prepared for.

There are many publications that provide advice and guidance for would-be ocean-crossing navigators, but without doubt the most comprehensive are the British Admiralty Volume 136 'Ocean Passages of the World' and the US 'Pilot Chart Atlases' (National Imagery and Mapping Agency).

OCEAN CURRENTS

The movements of the oceans can be a major factor influencing a deep-sea passage. Around the circumference of all major oceans there are significant currents, while towards the polar regions, strong ocean drifts sweep small vessels away like leaves in a millrace. The constant trade winds of the Northern and Southern Hemispheres also set up strong ocean drifts, which in turn create the equatorial currents and counter-currents. Any of these strong movements of water can influence

Opposite *Many of the hazards of crossing the oceans have been reduced with satellite communication and accurate weather forecasting.*

the passage of a yacht significantly and must be taken into account when planning the voyage.

First step in this planning is to study ocean current charts in order to know what currents the boat may encounter, what effect they will have and how to use, avoid or counter them.

Ocean current charts are produced by most hydrographic offices as well as private publishers, and most contain a great deal of information about the direction of flow, speed, seasonal changes and any other aspects that may influence the normal movement of the current.

A line drawn across the chart to represent the boat's proposed track will indicate if and where one of the major currents is likely to be encountered, and from this the effect on the boat's progress can be assessed. If the speed and direction of the flow are given, a fairly accurate estimate of its possible effect can be calculated by a simple vector diagram.

FINDING THE CURRENT

Currents have been described as rivers in the sea, which is quite a good analogy. But unlike rivers on land, which are firmly restricted by their banks, ocean currents have no restriction and their limits are, at best, flexible. The edge of the current may not always be where the chart indicates; indeed it may be some considerable distance away. Similarly, it may be wider or narrower than anticipated, and flow at a faster or slower rate. While the information on the current chart may be accurate in a general sense, in practice the navigator must determine just where the current begins and ends, and having found it, determine its characteristics and how it will affect the boat's track.

Water temperature is the key factor in dealing with currents. Some boats crossing an ocean will carry a sea temperature bucket and a thermometer, or have an electronic instrument that indicates sea temperature.

Right *An electronic sea temperature readout eliminates the need to keep dropping a bucket over the side!*

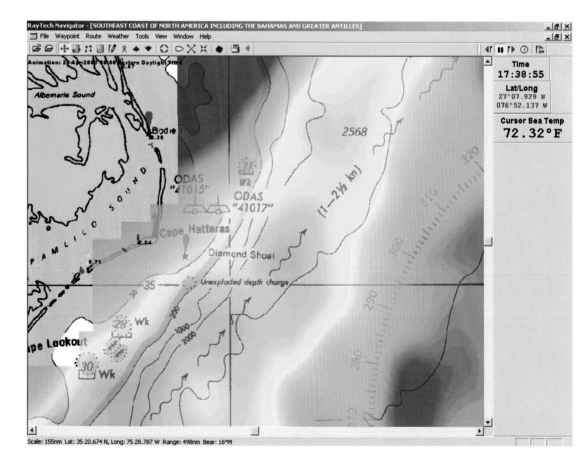

This bucket is usually just a canvas tube closed off at one end and with a hinged lid at the other, which allows water in but prevents it from flopping out. The bucket is dropped over the side, retrieved and the thermometer inserted. A distinct rise or fall in temperature will almost certainly indicate the presence of a current boundary, and the current chart will help identify it. While crossing the North Atlantic, for example, a distinct rise in sea temperature will indicate that the boat has entered the Gulf Stream, while farther north the Labrador Current, with its threat of icebergs, will make itself known when the sea temperature falls.

A daily reading of the sea-water temperature should be part of the navigator's routine at sea, so that the currents and their effects can be tracked.

CURRENT PATTERNS

Unlike tides, which ebb and flow, most currents run continuously in one direction. The northern sections of the Atlantic and Pacific Oceans have clockwise revolving currents, or 'gyres', as they are called. While the flow is consistently circulating around each ocean, it may vary in strength depending on a number of factors such as the effect of land masses, changes in underwater topography or merging with other currents, which may enhance or counter the main flow.

Most of these big currents are fairly slow moving, but as they extend over large areas, they can affect the progress of the boat quite considerably over the time it takes to sail through them. One of the important aspects of planning the route of a voyage is to determine whether or not to detour around an area affected by an unfavourable current or attempt to hitch a ride on a favourable current.

In the Southern Hemisphere the big oceans have a similar flow around the outer edges, but this time in an anti-clockwise direction. In the lower latitudes of the Southern Hemisphere, these circular currents sweep into the big Westerly Drift that runs around the globe unchecked by a land mass. Sailing from east to west in those latitudes would be like trying to walk to wrong way on an escalator. Similar problems would be encountered sailing against any of the smaller,

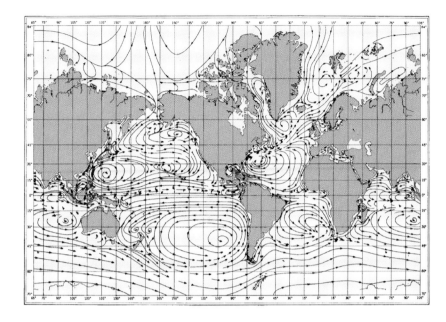

albeit fiercer, currents such as the Agulhas Current up the east coast of South Africa or the Humboldt Current down the west coast of South America.

Another major current that needs to be taken into account is the Equatorial Current, which is divided into two sections – north and south – and runs westward across the world in equatorial latitudes of the Pacific and Atlantic oceans. It is created by the trade winds of the Northern and Southern Hemispheres combining with the circular effect of the ocean movement to exacerbate the westerly flow in those regions. It is significant because it occurs partly in the windless doldrums, where vessels becalmed by the prevailing wind conditions will have difficulty countering any adverse effect it may have. An easterly counter-current runs between the North and South Equatorial Current, usually close to the equator itself.

These are the major ocean currents, but there are many smaller, yet still significant, currents in other areas of the world, which must be taken into consideration when planning a passage through waters that might be affected by them. The seasonal monsoons of the Indian Ocean can flow differently at different times of the year, while the Oyashio Current brings cold water from the Bering Strait, down the Siberian coast to Japan.

Above *The constant circulation of the main ocean currents has been well observed and can therefore be plotted and supplied to navigators in chart form.*

OCEAN WINDS

As with currents, the major wind patterns, created mostly by earth's rotation and pressure systems, have a considerable influence on the planning of an ocean passage.

Since few motor yachts are able to cross long stretches of ocean due to the lack of fuelling points, sailing craft are the main ocean travellers and, of course, the wind is of the utmost importance to them. When combined with an adverse current, a head wind can play havoc with progress and it requires careful planning to avoid such problems and route around areas where such winds and currents exist.

By the same token, favourable winds and currents can make the journey faster and more pleasant, and experienced ocean navigators seek out routes that provide the quickest and easiest passages.

The major surface winds follow consistent patterns, which make route plotting fairly easy.

THE TRADE WINDS

So named because they offered the old sailing ships fair winds to pursue their global trades, these winds are mainly created by hot air rising in the tropics and drawing in colder air from the higher latitudes.

As they flow inward toward the equator from north and south, these winds are deflected by the earth's rotation so that they blow from the southeast in the Southern Hemisphere and from the northeast in the Northern Hemisphere. They are named accordingly.

The trade winds are confined mostly to tropical areas but may be encountered farther north in midyear and farther south during the southern summer as they follow the sun on its seasonal travels. For the most part they are moderate (12–16 knots) to fresh (15–20 knots) in strength but consistent in direction, offering fast, pleasant sailing for those who can use them.

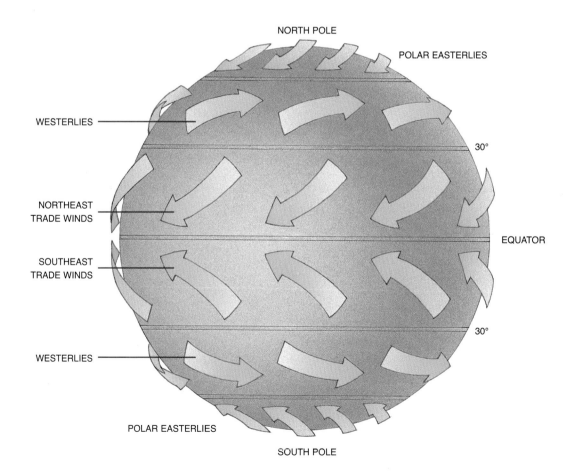

Right *The world's prevailing wind patterns play a great part in the movement of ocean currents, as well as providing motive power for ocean-crossing sailors.*

THE WESTERLIES

In the middle to high latitudes of both hemispheres, the prevailing westerlies are the main wind feature. This is particularly the case in the Southern Ocean, where a belt of strong westerly winds blow continuously around the world.

The rugged western coastlines of Ireland and Scotland bear witness to the westerly Atlantic gales, while in the southern regions, the winds of the 'Roaring Forties' strike fear into the heart of all sailors as they sweep towards the infamous Cape Horn. These winds can build up enormous seas, with the giant rollers of the Southern Ocean growing bigger and bigger as they race around the world, unchecked by any land mass.

It would obviously be futile for any yacht seeking a fast and safe passage to work against these winds. Sailing before them is a better option, and the old wool and grain clippers made phenomenal speeds racing westward in order to be 'first around the Horn'. However, those were big ships, and capable of handling the monstrous seas in those latitudes where even sizeable yachts can quickly come to grief.

THE DOLDRUMS

Also to be avoided where possible, but for a totally different reason, the doldrums consist of a belt of very light winds and calms around the tropical latitudes in every ocean. They lie between the trade winds and offer little in the form of predictable wind or weather. While traditionally an area with little or no wind, the unstable air masses of the tropics can produce almost anything from sudden storms to tropical cyclones, as well as the calms that frustrated the old sailing ships and continue to frustrate modern sailors.

Unfortunately, the doldrums are not as easily avoided as the other wind systems, since they occur in every major ocean, spanning every route that crosses the equator or comes near it.

EQUATORIAL CURRENTS AND COUNTER-CURRENTS

The trade winds in both northern and southern oceans create a strong current that flows in a westerly direction above and below the equator in each hemisphere. Between these two westerly currents, a counter-current runs in an easterly direction.

TROPICAL REVOLVING STORMS

Better known by their 'trade' names of hurricane (Caribbean and South Atlantic), typhoon (China Sea and North Pacific) and cyclone (South Pacific and Indian Ocean), these are the feared 'rogue' storms in which winds reach phenomenal strengths.

The disastrous damage and loss of life that occurs when one of these storms hits the land is well known indeed, yet their potential for damage is even greater in the open sea where they are at their peak. Even large ocean-going ships are in danger when caught by a Tropical Revolving Storm (TRS).

To a certain extent these storms are predictable, in that they always form over water in tropical or near

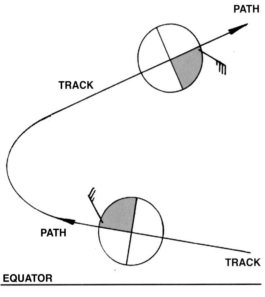

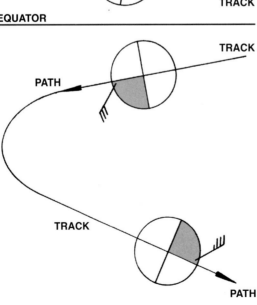

Right *Tropical Revolving Storms are usually fairly predictable, following paths that curve north-ward from equatorial regions in the Northern Hemisphere and southward from the equator in the Southern Hemisphere. The shaded areas indicate the most dangerous segment of the storm.*

tropical latitudes and at certain times of the year. In the Northern Hemisphere the danger period is from August to November and in the Southern Hemisphere from December to April.

However, it is not unknown for them to also occur outside these limits, and cyclone, hurricane or typhoon watches are usually kept well into the non-danger period. During the season, warnings are broadcast continuously from the moment a storm forms and it is tracked by radar, aircraft and satellite in order to monitor its progress.

Tropical revolving storms are also predictable in their make-up and their movement.

Like a giant whirlpool of air, these winds rotate at high speed around an 'eye' or core – clockwise in the Southern Hemisphere, anti-clockwise in the Northern Hemisphere – the whole whirling mass moving initially westward through a tropical region, then curling away to the south and southeast in the Southern Hemisphere and to the north and northeast in the Northern Hemisphere.

The eye may be fairly small, but the extreme winds that race around it can reach speeds of more than 250km (156 miles) per hour.

The storms tend to break up if they pass over land, and degrade to a normal rain depression (low-pressure system) when they leave the tropics. In the meantime, of course, they will have wrought havoc along their track.

While these storms are carefully monitored and radio warnings issued the moment there are signs of one developing, slow-moving yachts crossing an ocean can sometimes be caught unawares, either through failure to pick up the warnings or just being in the wrong place at the wrong time. There is no alternative for a boat in the path of TRS but to get out of its way as quickly as possible, and by any means possible.

In order to determine the best moves to make, it is important to first determine the location of the storm relative to the boat. Radio warnings from storm centres may advise on the position and movement of the TRS, otherwise unmistakable signs both in the sea and the sky will indicate its approach:

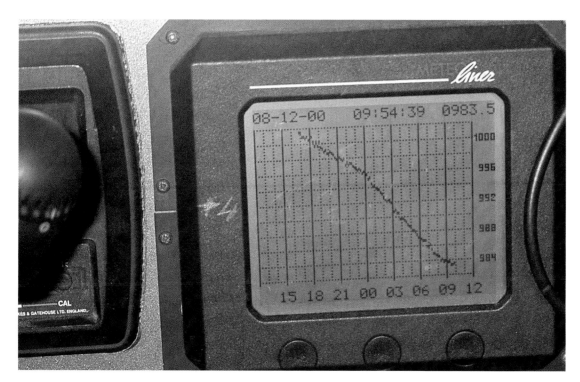

Left *One of the most significant indications of an approaching Tropical Revolving Storm is a rapid and deep fall in the barometer reading.*

- The barometer falls fast to an exceptionally low reading.
- A heavy ground swell, quite distinct from normal swell, sets in.
- The sky takes on a distinctly lurid appearance. The wind develops an eerie 'banshee' howl, quite unlike any noise made by normal winds.
- The wind begins to shift markedly as the tropical storm approaches.

The following procedures will help determine the location of the storm in relation to the boat. Since its path is reasonably predictable, the best way to get out of its path can then be assessed:

- Face directly into the wind.
- The centre of the storm lies 10 points (112°) to the left (in the Southern Hemisphere) or right (in the Northern Hemisphere).
- From this direction, plot the probable path of the storm as described earlier, and locate the boat's position in relation to the storm's track.
- Head the boat out of the path of the storm, preferably toward the equator, unless this will bring you closer to the storm. Always bear in mind that the storm's probable track will curve to the north (in the Northern Hemisphere) and south (in the Southern Hemisphere).

OTHER WINDS

There are many other wind and weather conditions that affect boats at sea; the remarkably consistent land and sea breeze is a good example. But such winds are mostly experienced in waters close to land masses and are not specifically related to the open oceans.

Global winds are mostly encountered in the open ocean where they are unhampered by land masses and blow over long distances.

Left *The chances of surviving a TRS in a yacht or small craft are virtually nil.*

Right top *On a Mercator chart, which is most useful for navigation, the shortest distance between two points (a great circle) is shown as a curve.*

Right bottom *On a Gnomonic chart, the great circle route appears straight.*

Below *Meridians of Longitude are great circles and thus appear on a chart as straight lines, as does the equator. All other straight lines on a chart, including parallels of latitude, follow a curved path across the earth's surface. The curve is toward the poles.*

GREAT CIRCLE SAILING

The shortest distance between two points on an ocean Mercator chart is not a straight line – it is a curve known as a 'great circle', which becomes a straight line on a Gnomonic chart.

If the line were drawn between the same two points on the earth's surface and then the earth's surface flattened out to make a chart, the straight line would become a curve, because it was originally drawn on a curved surface. It may seem that there is not a great deal of difference in distance along the curve of a great circle compared to the straight (rhumb) line, and indeed this is the case in certain directions. But over the long distance of an ocean passage and in most directions, there can be a considerable difference.

The definition of a great circle is 'a circle whose plane passes through the centre of the earth'. The meridians of longitude, for example, are great circles since, like the segments of an orange, their plane passes through the centre of the orange. Similarly the equator is a great circle, but other parallels of latitude are not. The higher the latitude, the greater the discrepancy in distance between a great circle track and a rhumb line track.

THE GNOMONIC CHART

One way of resolving the problem of the Great Circle would be to create a curved chart representing the earth's surface, but this is a practical impossibility.

However, a specially constructed chart, called a Gnomonic chart, creates the nearest solution and provides a means of plotting curved great circle tracks on the normal navigation (Mercator) chart. Because of its already curved configuration, a straight line between departure and arrival positions on a Gnomonic chart represents the great circle track and thus the shortest distance for the boat to travel.

This track can then be transposed onto a normal Mercator chart.

Gnomonic charts can be obtained from any chart agent and the procedure for plotting a great circle track is as follows:

- Plot the latitude and longitude of departure and arrival positions on the gnomonic chart, then join them with a straight line.
- Since it is difficult for a boat to sail a curving course, waypoints must be selected, usually where the line crosses meridians of longitude – say at each 10° of longitude.

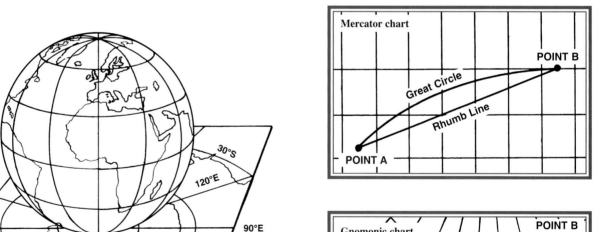

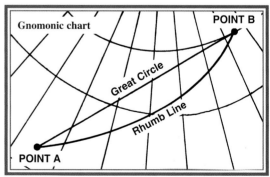

- Transfer the latitude and longitude of each way-point from the Gnomonic to the Mercator ocean chart being used.
- When all the waypoints have been plotted on the Mercator chart, join the departure position to the first waypoint and then transfer it to the nearest compass rose. The first course to steer can be read off.
- Continue along the track, joining each waypoint to the next and recording the course between them.
- When the final course has been recorded, you will then need to plot the great circle track on the chart. Each course to follow – from waypoint to way-point – will then need to be converted to a compass course for the boat to steer.
- On arrival the boat will have effectively steered the shortest distance from departure position. However, bear in mind that when sailing, wind directions dictate the course and a great circle course may become impractical.

COMMUNICATION

As anyone who has been out there will tell you, the ocean is a lonely place. Not only are you physically alone, but once well away from the shore, communication with other people can be spasmodic, sometimes difficult, sometimes impossible.

This is not a good situation at best, and when things turn nasty, and when you desperately need help, poor communication can be life threatening.

Fortunately, modern electronics have in recent years made great strides in reducing the difficulty of communication over long distances, and the introduction of satellite communication has advanced that progress to the point where given good equipment and reasonable atmospheric and weather conditions, no boat should be out of touch with the world for any lengthy period, if at all.

More importantly, systems have been put in place so that when an emergency arises, there is always some way in which a distress message can be successfully transmitted.

The major communication systems are now mostly reliant on satellites, although VHF (Very

High Frequency) radio is still widely used for short-range communication and SSB (Single Side Band) radio is used by small craft for longer range communication. But the reliability and ease of use of the satellite-based systems is such that SSB is fast becoming replaced by the UHF (Ultra High Frequency) satellite systems.

Above *Satellite and radio communications demand so many antennae that the deckhouse of a well-equipped boat can resemble a small forest.*

VHF RADIO

Most basic of all electronic communication systems, VHF is a 'line-of-sight' radio system with an average range of around 20–35 nautical miles depending on height or design of the antenna and their power output. The curvature of the earth is the main restricting factor for this radio system, although its convenience makes it popular for short-distance work.

Right A typical VHF radio unit, which includes a Public Address system.

Centre This illustrates the use of satellites for the Inmarsat system.

Below Modern communications systems range from line-of-sight VHF to global-spanning Inmarsat. So compact are these units that even small craft can carry a wide range of systems.

CELLPHONE

Cellphones, or mobile phones, also have line-of-sight limitations, although this can be improved in basic cellphones by mounting a cellular antenna at the masthead or using greater transmitting power. More powerful cellphones with special antennae can be hooked into satellite systems to provide a wide range of communications including voice, fax and data services that can be interfaced with on-board computers to provide internet facilities.

The only problem with the cellphone communication system is the different standards used by different countries. This system is inoperable if the cellphone is not compatible with the shore standard.

SINGLE SIDE BAND

Operating either with medium frequency (MF) or high frequency (HF), this radio system covers far greater distances than VHF and can span the globe.

This was the popular system for ocean-crossing boats for many years, but it proved vulnerable to poor atmospheric and weather conditions and has lost popularity because of more reliable satellite systems.

INTERNATIONAL MARITIME SATELLITE CORPORATION

Abbreviated to 'Inmarsat', this refers to a group of communication companies that operate the major satellite communications systems. A terminal aboard

the boat connects to an orbiting satellite, which in turn connects with a land-based station. Through this system, voice communications can be transmitted to shore and then into the normal civilian telephone system.

There are a number of Inmarsat transceivers on the market designed to cope with different levels of communication and the network covers most of the world, other than the polar regions. The most useful of the systems for small craft is the Mini-M, manufactured and sold under a number of different brand names.

DIGITAL SELECTIVE CALLING

Abbreviated to DSC, this is a system that uses encoded radio signals to send radio messages on VHF, MF or HF to selected vessels while excluding others.

SAFETY

Communication with the shore or with other vessels is essential when an emergency arises.

Before 1999, most emergency procedures involved the use of normal voice communication by radio and the well-known Mayday call as the signal for distress.

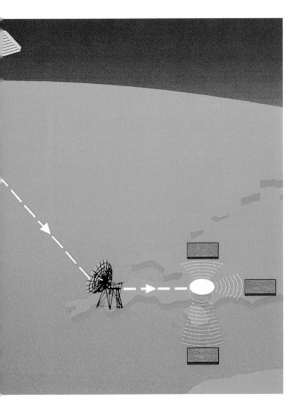

Left *The 'Man Overboard Button': once activated, it alerts the electronic navigation system of the emergency, and stores the lat/long position of the boat.*

While this system is still extensively used in small craft, in 1999 an international system called Global Maritime Distress and Safety System (GMDSS) was introduced, which revolutionised the whole approach to maritime safety. The system divides the sea into four areas:

Sea Area A1

Sea Area A1 extends from the coastline to 20 miles (32km) offshore, which is mostly within range of VHF stations with DSC capability.

Sea Area A2

Sea Area A2 covers the offshore waters between 20 and 100 miles (32 and 160km) from the coast, within range of MF or HF stations employing DSC.

Sea Area A3

Sea Area A3 extends from the 100-mile (160-km) outer limit of Sea Area 2 across the oceans between the latitudes of 70° north and 70° south; an area covered by the Inmarsat communications satellites.

Sea Area A4

Sea Area A4 covers the remaining sea areas.

Vessels in each sea area are required to carry items of safety communications equipment necessary in that area, including Emergency Position Indicating Radio Beacons (EPIRB) and other safety items.

Although yachts and small craft are not obliged to carry this equipment, it would be an unwise skipper who put to sea without the minimum requirements. Details of these requirements can be obtained from chandlers, chart agents or nautical bookshops.

MARITIME SAFETY INFORMATION

Broadcast at regular intervals, Maritime Safety Information (MSI) communicates navigational and meteorological warnings, forecasts, search and rescue notices and other relevant safety information. It is transmitted through Navtex and Safety Net.

Navtex

Navtex is distributed to inshore waters through a network of coast radio stations. It does not use voice messages but provides a printout from the ship's on-board receiver.

Safety Net

Safety Net sends MSI across the open seas through the Inmarsat network. It covers all areas except the polar regions.

EMERGENCY

Despite all the modern communication and safety innovations, not all yachts and small craft are able to use them. Fortunately, the many and varied traditional methods of calling for help in an emergency still hold good.

Below *Elements of the GMDSS system: satellites are located around the globe at strategic points, to provide a complete system of communications (including weather, fax and internet requirements) for vessels across all oceans.*

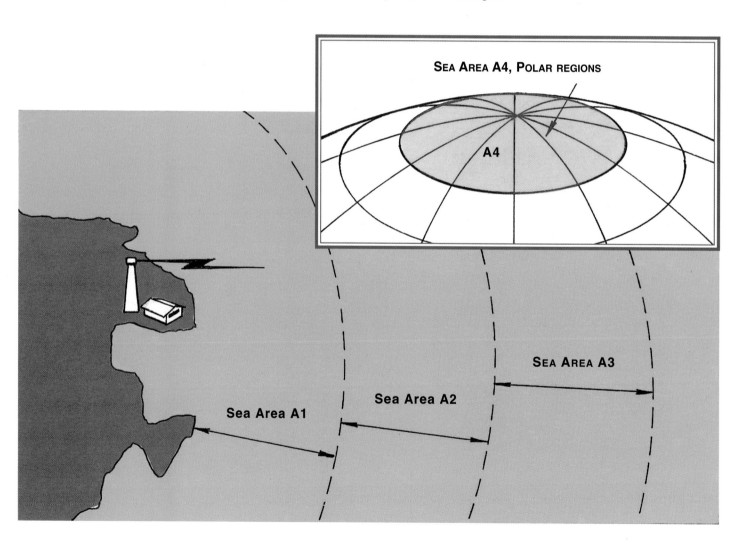

SEA AREA A4, POLAR REGIONS

A4

SEA AREA A3

Sea Area A2

Sea Area A1

Left *The sailor's lifeline: the EPIRB communicates with a satellite the minute it is activated, which indicates its position sometimes to within a boat's length! Personal EPIRBs, which are attached to lifejackets, can be of enormous assistance in locating a person overboard in the water.*

Below *At times like this the EPIRB can be the difference between life and death, as it enables rescue teams to pinpoint the boat's position and save wasted time searching the surrounding sea.*

- Set off an EPIRB. This will trigger responses in shore bases, search-and-rescue (SAR) services, COSPAS/SARSAT satellites and aircraft.
- The spoken word 'Mayday', repeated three times on VHF channel 16 or 2182 on SSB, or, if necessary, on any other frequency, followed by details of the vessel's name, position and the nature of the emergency. (Mayday comes from the French 'M'aidez' – help me – the international spoken signal of distress in extreme emergency.)
- If the emergency is not life threatening, use the word 'Pan-Pan' instead of Mayday.
- Releasing flares, smoke signals, rockets or smoke from a bucket of burning rags.
- Morse SOS by light, sound or radio.
- The slow raising and lowering of outstretched arms.
- Releasing a distinctly coloured dye into the water.
- The sounding of a gun or foghorn.
- Flying/displaying square and round shapes next to each other.

ELECTRONIC NAVIGATION

One of the first electronic aids to navigation was the echo sounder, which transmitted an electronic pulse from the underside of the boat and measured the time it took to bounce off the sea bottom, thus indicating the depth of water.

After World War II, with the discovery of radar, electronic navigation developed in leaps and bounds. Probably the biggest leap was in 1960 when SATNAV, the first satellite navigation system, was tested. By 1996 a totally new satellite system was in place, providing navigators with a user-friendly yet remarkably accurate method of position fixing. The Global Positioning System (GPS), as it is called, provides simplicity and accuracy to a degree only dreamed of before.

THE GLOBAL POSITIONING SYSTEM

A Global Positioning System employs a somewhat similar system to sextant sights in terms of plotting the boat's position. A sextant altitude of a star provides a circle of position and the boat is located somewhere on that circle. When three stars are taken and three circles plotted, the intersection of all three is the position of the boat.

In the electronic system, GPS satellites replace the stars and provide a similar series of circles on earth's surface, which also intersect to provide the boat's position.

There are between 26 and 30 satellites in the GPS system, orbiting the earth every 12 hours, and usually 24 are actively in use. By computing the time it takes for the satellite signal to reach the boat's antenna, the GPS receiver measures the

Opposite *For immediate reference and convenience, most navigation and sailing instruments have readout or repeater dials in the cockpit.*

distance between the boat and the satellite. From this a circle of position is computed and crossed with others to provide the position of the boat on earth's surface to a remarkable degree of accuracy – often within a boat length!

And GPS can do far more than just locate the boat's position. It can provide almost instant information on a wide range of subjects. It can calculate the boat's speed, course, direction and any factors influencing its progress, such as current and tide.

When integrated with other electronic systems it can provide a 'moving picture' of the boat's progress across an electronic chart.

GPS RECEIVERS

The GPS receiver is the 'brain' of the system, containing a computer that determines which satellites can be used, receiving information from them and then processing their data to provide the boat's position. The early GPS receivers provided a digital

readout of latitude and longitude, and this is still an option in modern receivers, although the trend nowadays is to display the boat as an icon (usually an arrow) on an electronic chart.

ANTENNAE

The wavelength of the satellite signal is very short, so relatively small antennas can be used.

Some hand-held receivers have a patch antenna (a small portable antenna); it works best when it is held parallel to the horizon. Others have a quad-helix or loopstick antenna (a fitted antenna more commonly used with larger GPS sets), which is more sensitive to low-elevation satellites.

However, the best result is obtained with a stabilized external dome antenna (with a rotating dish antenna), since the GPS operates most efficiently when it has a clear line-of-sight to the sky and is not obstructed by the boat's superstructure, masts and rigging, or even the user's body.

Below *The layout of a fully integrated electronic navigation network for a yacht or small vessel.*

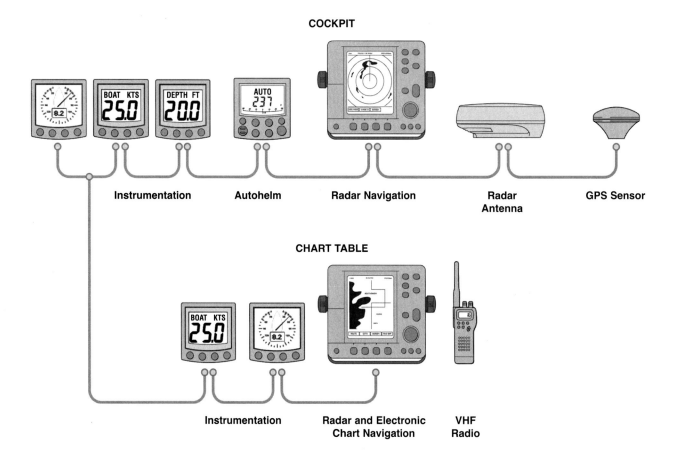

START-UP

Before a newly installed GPS receiver can be used, it should be initialized by entering the date and time together with the approximate latitude and longitude of the boat's position. These need only be approximate – to the nearest whole degree – as the receiver will sort it out as it 'warms up'. Failure to initialize properly will not prevent the set from operating, but it will take some minutes to activate – a process known as 'cold start'.

Some of the latest receivers do not require this warm-up period; the manufacturer will advise on this. Once 'warmed-up', the receiver stores information in its memory, which enables it to restart quickly after being switched off. However, leaving it switched off for more than two weeks or moving it more than 300 miles (480km) from where it was last used can result in another cold start.

CHART DATUM

The latitude and longitude of a plot on a paper chart may sometimes not correspond to the same latitude and longitude provided by GPS. The older paper charts – now being updated – were drawn from surveys done with systems less accurate than GPS.

Such errors can be significant, and it is important to check a paper chart being used for GPS plots to ensure that it is drawn to the current WGS (World Geodetic Survey) datum, which is compatible with GPS, and not one of the older datum. If they are different, a correction must be applied and this will be indicated on the chart.

DIFFERENTIAL GPS

The incredible accuracy of GPS prompted the nervous US military to restrict its availability to non-military users. A deliberately degraded system, but still with an accuracy of at least 20m (65ft), was provided for amateur yacht navigators and commercial vessels.

However, a technique called 'differential navigation' was devised, which improved the accuracy of the standard system, and this is now widely available in coastal areas, known as Differential GPS (DGPS).

A series of GPS reference stations are located around the major continents, which compare their known position against a computed GPS position, and transmit a correction factor to the boat's GPS, providing accuracy often to around 10m (32ft). Many GPS receivers are DGPS-compatible or have an additional antenna to cater for this system.

While the US has abandoned its 'selective availability' policy, the DGPS network is still widely used.

Buyers of a new GPS need not be concerned if it is not equipped with DGPS, for the standard, good-quality GPS is capable of providing completely accurate results providing it is calibrated and checked before being used on an open sea passage.

Such strides have been made in the development of GPS and other electronic systems over the past years that mariners can enjoy the accuracy of navigation previously reserved for naval and commercial ships.

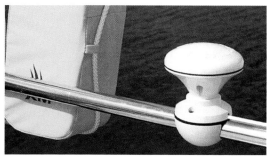

Left Most GPS units require only a small antenna that must be mounted outside the hull and cabin in order to obtain a clear 'view' of the sky. Hand-held GPS units, like cellphones, must be taken out on deck for the same reason.

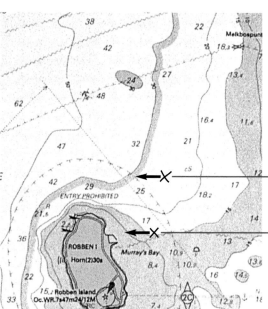

Left The GPS is so accurate that older charts, surveyed by less accurate means, may reveal errors when using GPS to plot positions. A datum correction must be applied in order to allow accurate plotting.

Your GPS lat and long indicates that you are here.

But after applying the datum correction you find that you are actually here.

THE ELECTRONIC COMPASS

Although the magnetic compass is still the mainstay of all small-boat navigation, electronic compasses have become more popular in recent years. Previously, their main drawback was the unsuitable environment on board small craft, the relatively high cost of installation and their requirement for continuous power supply.

As with all technology, these drawbacks are gradually being overcome, although the latest laser compasses are still expensive.

THE GYRO COMPASS

The gyro compass has been fitted in large naval and commercial ships for well over half a century, yet only in recent years has it been adapted to small craft, and then in a limited way.

It is a superb compass, which eliminates the errors associated with the magnetic compass and provides a true reading that can be drawn on or taken off a chart without worrying about variation and deviation, even in steel vessels. However, the high cost of the gyro has always been a factor against it gaining popularity in small craft.

Below *The gyro compass is based on the principle of a spinning top.*

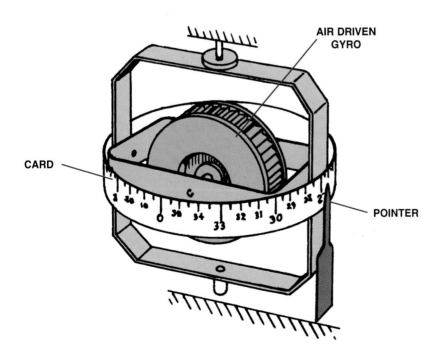

CARD

AIR DRIVEN GYRO

POINTER

A gyro works on the principle of a spinning top, which defies gravity and remains upright as long as it is spinning at high speed. Similarly the wheel or disk that is the heart of a gyro compass remains in position as long as it is spinning at high speed. The axis is set to point to north and providing it can move freely, it will remain pointing in that direction regardless of how the boat swings around it

The initial problem with fitting gyro compasses in small craft is, as mentioned, their high cost. In addition, the environment of a small boat is not well suited to such a sensitive instrument. The wild gyrations of a small boat in a big sea can upset the delicate balance of the instrument, and since most small craft rely on batteries for their power source, this does not provide the consistent and reliable power supply that is required to keep the gyro spinning.

OPTICAL GYRO COMPASS

The use of a laser beam instead of a spinning wheel, which is the latest development in electronic compasses, is attracting increasing attention.

There are two forms of optical gyros: the ring laser gyro (RLG) and the fibreoptic gyro (FOG). As they are both solid-state gyros, both have great advantages in that they have no moving parts, and are rugged and reliable.

These gyros operate on an optical principle called the 'Sagnac Effect', in which two light beams travel in opposite directions around a closed loop. The technical details are too complex to describe here, but, as its name implies, it is all literally 'done with mirrors' which create a ring of reflected light.

The ring laser gyro was the first to be brought into production, but is unwieldy, expensive and not suitable for small boat use.

A later development by the German Litef GmbH Corporation, called the 'fibreoptic gyro', offers a more compact unit using a fibreoptic coil to convey a modified semiconductor laser beam. The fibreoptic gyro has no moving parts, thus reducing or even eliminating many of the problems associated with normal gyro compasses, which makes them unsuitable for small craft. There may, however, still be problems when using a fibreoptic gyro in small craft in a big seaway. Although currently still expensive, its ruggedness and ability to withstand considerable motion without the need for gimbals or other protective fittings seem likely to make this the compass of the future for boats and small craft.

Already fitted in some aircraft, commercial vessels and larger motor yachts, production and marketing forces should soon bring the price down to reasonable levels. Then the term FOG may well have a different meaning for mariners!

FLUXGATE COMPASS

Often referred to as a 'digital' compass, this is a well-established electronic compass used by many small boat navigators around the world. Providing a digital readout enables many of the errors associated with the magnetic compass – including deviation – to be reduced or removed internally. This in turns means that a remote display can be mounted in the cockpit near the steering position while the fluxgate sensor unit can be located below decks where the movement of the boat and other adverse influences are reduced to a minimum.

This type of compass provides excellent accuracy. In addition, as the digital display is easy to read, the fluxgate compass is popular with small boat owners who find steering a straight course on a magnetic compass – with the boat charging around in a seaway – virtually impossible.

CALCULATORS

The great advantage of navigational calculators is avoiding the high risk of mathematical error in sight computations. Since the average boat owner is no mathematician, the possibility of getting sight computations right every time is not good. Calculators not only reduce the chance of error in the calculations but also make the work easier and quicker.

The sextant sight is taken and the altitude fed into the calculator together with other relevant data such as the GMT of sight, DR position, height of eye, and index error. By following the prompts, or the manufacturer's instructions, the azimuth and intercept

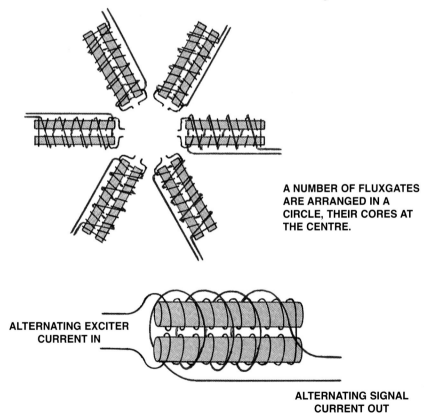

– in the case of a sight reduction computation – can be read off and plotted. These calculators are relatively inexpensive to purchase, very easy to use, and operate on small batteries. All in all they are exceptionally well suited to boat navigation.

Left The fluxgate compass provides an accurate and stable digital readout that makes the helmsman's job of steering the boat much easier.

Below The principle of the fluxgate element, which forms the basis of the most popular electronic compasses. It uses electronics to detect the earth's magnetic field, and depends on electromagnetic induction.

A NUMBER OF FLUXGATES ARE ARRANGED IN A CIRCLE, THEIR CORES AT THE CENTRE.

ALTERNATING EXCITER CURRENT IN

ALTERNATING SIGNAL CURRENT OUT

Above *Any navigator with a basic knowledge of personal computers is able to use one for navigational work – it is simply a matter of loading and learning the relevant software.*

Right *One of the most useful of all electronic aids to navigation, the electronic chart plotter can be integrated with a number of other instruments, thus providing a complete navigation system on a single display.*

ON-BOARD COMPUTERS

The development of laptop and hand-held computers suggests that it won't be long before computers are only a little larger than calculators.

While they do much the same job as calculators where sight computations are concerned, on-board computers have many additional features such as the ability to handle internet connections, weatherfax, email, Navtex (a navigational communications system for broadcasting information, almost like a seagoing fax) and a host of other useful services. And with the right software, racing tactics, boat management and spreadsheets can also be catered for, while those boring moments at sea can be relieved by multimedia offerings in the form of videos, movies and games!

Employing a PC for navigational work means simply loading the necessary software and then using whatever is required for a particular purpose. Like calculators, sight resolution requires only the basic sight information to be loaded, then 'following the prompt' is used to

obtain an azimuth and intercept. Tidal information, weather forecasts and maritime warnings can be downloaded as required, and information on the procedures for entering a port in a foreign country can be obtained in good time for the boarding officials.

THE ELECTRONIC CHART PLOTTER

Perhaps the most useful of all electronic instruments is the electronic chart plotter. Integrated with other navigation instruments it can create a complete command station with a single facility to cover all navigational requirements.

The plotter displays a marine chart, mostly in full colour, with the position of the vessel (from the GPS) usually indicated by an arrow.

All navigation is carried out on the screen by feeding in any required data and using menus, keys or trackball to compute it into a visual readout. A range of charts can be obtained, usually in a cartridge or on a compact disk (CD).

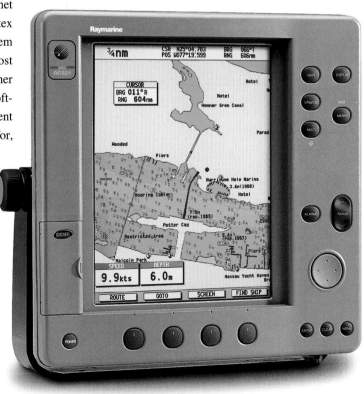

RASTER CHARTS

Raster charts are made by digital scanning of original paper charts at high resolution into a computer file. Their main advantage is that they appear on screen to exactly reflect the original paper chart and are therefore immediately familiar to the navigator.

Raster charts are generally quicker and cheaper to produce than other charts, but because the screening creates an image from dots (pixels), zooming in too severely can break up the image, while zooming out too far can induce a fuzzy outline.

VECTOR CHARTS

These charts are created by an electronic process known as 'heads-up digitizing'. Using a raster image as a backdrop, vectors (representing map features as locational points, lines or polygons) of selected features on a map are created. In other words, vector charts are not screened from paper charts but use direct data import to build up the required detail that will display a fully electronic chart with no paper

chart used in the process. The many 'layers' of information on a vector chart provide increasing levels of detail without sacrificing image resolution.

There are a number of electronic chart manufacturers of which the C-Map and Navionics companies are the most prominent.

SEAMLESS CHARTS

Charts are displayed in one of two systems: individual charts, where the plotter automatically loads the next chart when the edge of one is reached; or a 'seamless' system, where all charts are stored in a single data base. In this case the edges of the chart are eliminated and the navigator can move effortlessly from one chart to the next without interruption and regardless of scale.

Left centre The electronic chart display is similar to that of the old paper charts. Indeed, some types of plotter use electronically scanned paper charts for their display.

Below Raster (top) and vector (bottom) chart displays. Note that the vector display is less cluttered than the raster display.

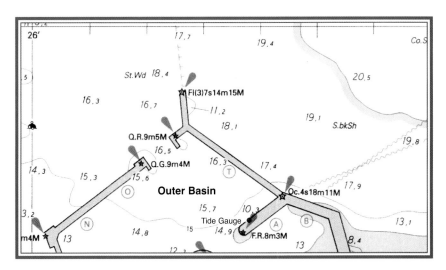

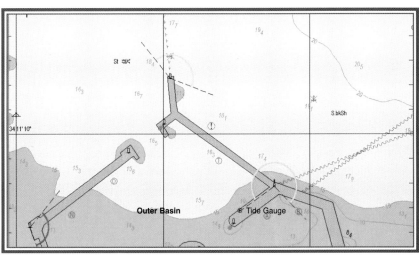

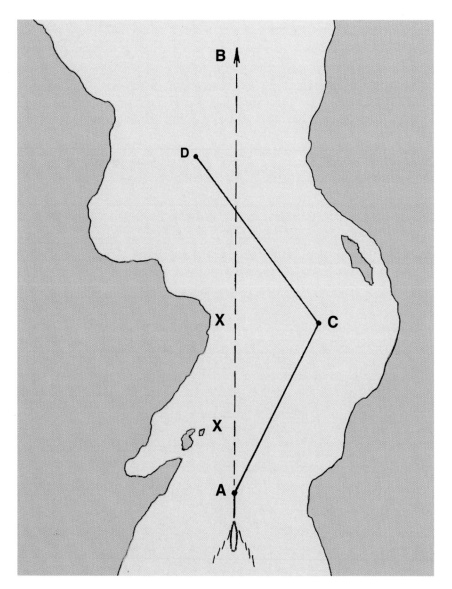

WAYPOINT NAVIGATION

When navigating from one point to another on an electronic chart, there is no need to plot a departure position since the plotter is interfaced with the boat's GPS and the arrow indicating the boat's position appears when the plotter is switched on. By moving the cursor to the predetermined arrival position and pressing 'enter', the arrival position is established as a waypoint, and a course to steer from departure to waypoint can then be read off. If the plotter is integrated with the autohelm, the boat will start to steer that course immediately.

The waypoint can also be entered as a latitude and longitude position, or it can be stored in the plotter's memory from a previous occasion, in which case it can be recalled by pressing the 'go to' button. When a complex course is required, a series of courses is laid off from waypoint to waypoint, just as it is in traditional coastal navigation (see page 57). Each time the boat has to make an alteration of course to avoid a hazard or round a headland, a waypoint is established. In this manner the entire route can be prepared and entered into the system before leaving the departure position.

Some integrated systems will automatically direct the autopilot to change course at each waypoint, some will need the 'go to' button to be pressed to direct the boat onto the next course.

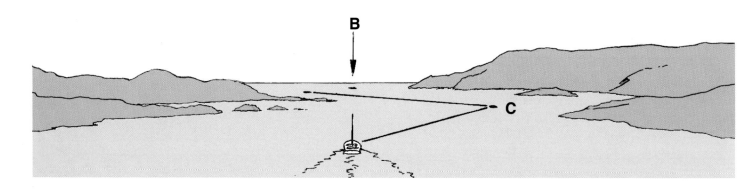

Many of the better units sound an alarm if the boat gets too close to a hazard, or if she wanders too far off her course line. This latter is known as cross track error (XTE) and can be preset to ensure that the boat follows the most accurate course. Set, drift and leeway can be programmed into the unit, so that once underway and interfaced with the autopilot, the navigator has little more to do than keep an eye on the boat's progress. Since the GPS updates the boat's position every second, her location is constantly monitored and shown on the screen, while information such as Course over the Ground (COG), Course Made Good (CMG), Speed Over the Ground (SOG), Cross Track Error (XTE) and any other relevant information are constantly displayed or can be called up at the press of a button.

Most modern plotters can display more than one window at a time, so that a check can be kept on what is happening without changing the screen. For example, while tracking the boat's progress on the electronic chart, other windows can duplicate the display on the sounder and radar screens. More sophisticated units will overlay the radar screen on the chart, providing the ultimate 'moving picture' of the boat's progress.

Zoom facilities allow chart features to be enlarged for more detail or reduced to bring in more of the surrounding area. Distances can be measured and bearings taken by moving the cursor and pressing a button, while most chart programmes provide tidal passage information that indicates time and flow of tides along the route and at waypoints.

One of the most important features is a man overboard facility (MOB), which instantly calculates the return course to the person in the water, allowing for tide, wind and sea conditions.

Above *Split-screen displays enable a number of electronic instruments to be used at the same time on one display, such as Radar, GPS, log and sounder.*

Opposite *The principle of waypoint navigation: while point A to point B might at first appear to be a mid-channel course, it brings the boat close to dangerous Point X. By assigning waypoints C and D, the navigator is able to take the boat through a true – and safe – mid-channel route.*

These are but a few of the features that are available with top-line chart plotters. Depending on the manufacture and the degree of sophistication, the capability of some instruments is astonishing. The Raytech Navigator, for example, can display animated tide stations and currents overlaid on the chart; use wind speed and direction and current data to compute optimal ocean routes and display them on the chart; analyze the boat's performance on a graph; and, using the dimensions of the boat's sails, display actual and optimal performance for racing crews.

Right *In a radar system, it is the quality of the scanner that determines the quality of the image. This is an example of a long-range Open Array radar scanner.*

Below *Radar is essentially an electronic map of everything surrounding the boat. In this way, even in a fog, the navigator has a good idea what is going on around the vessel.*

RADAR

The 'seeing eye' of radar has been a boon to sailors of all kinds since the end of World War 11.

An electronic pulse, transmitted from a rotating antenna on the boat, bounces back off any solid object it encounters, and the returning 'echo' is picked up and translated into a map of the sea around the vessel, displayed on a CRT (Cathode Ray Tube) or LCD (Liquid Crystal Display) screen in the navigator's compartment. The display places the boat at the centre of the screen, with the surrounding features of sea, land and shipping traffic around it in what is effectively a moving map.

Radar cannot see over the horizon, so it is important to place the antenna as high as possible. Some radar units have a range of over 70 nautical miles (130km), providing the transmitting power and height of the antenna are suitable.

Keys or buttons and a trackball provide the controls for operating the unit; distances can be measured on the screen by a variable range marker (VRM) or fixed range rings, and an electronic bearing cursor indicates bearings. Usually the vessel's heading is at the top of the screen, but interface with a compass can give it a 'north up' aspect. The display may be in colour or monochrome and can be integrated into a complete navigational network, integrating with fluxgate compass, sounder, chart plotter and distance log to provide a complete navigation station.

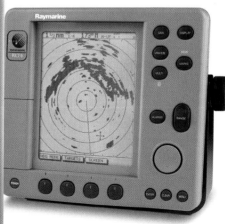

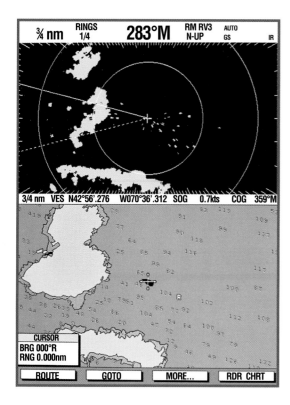

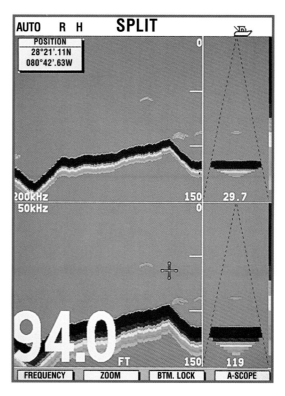

ERRORS

Although modern radar sets are normally accurate and trouble-free, some errors can arise in use and the operator needs to take these into consideration. Where a rocky cliff face will give a strong echo that appears clearly on the display, a low sandy beach or marshy swamp will not reflect the pulse as strongly, and will produce only a faint echo on the screen, sometimes no image at all.

Similarly, radar cannot see round corners, so hazards hidden behind headlands or obstructions will not show up on the display. If there is something in front of the antenna (a mast, for example), a blind spot may be created, and this must be rectified by swinging the boat's head from side to side occasionally.

In a big seaway, small objects such as fishing boats and yachts can disappear in the trough between waves or return a very weak, spasmodic echo, which might not be easily seen. To avoid this problem, boats sailing in busy shipping areas should fit a radar reflector high up on the vessel, which will return a strong echo when hit by a radar pulse.

RAMARK AND RACON

Because radar is so widely used, most navigational buoys and beacons carry radar reflectors.

However, at the entrance to a port there may be dozens of buoys and beacons and the navigator will have difficulty distinguishing one from the other on the screen. To overcome this, major buoys are equipped with an electronic device, called a Racon beacon, that enables them to be identified.

The Racon beacon emits a coded signal (Ramark) in the radar frequency when it is struck by a radar pulse. It appears on the radar screen as a series of dashes radiating out of the buoy.

The Ramark identifying signal is also a series of dashes (or dots) radiating along a bearing from the buoy to the centre of the radar screen. Unlike Racon, this signal is not triggered when struck by a radar pulse, but operates continuously.

So useful is this system that most major ports around the world, especially those where bad weather is common, are equipped with Racon and Ramark to provide all-weather access to shipping.

ELECTRONIC NAVIGATION

Right and opposite bottom

The steering wheel or tiller of the craft can be electronically integrated with an autohelm and other electronic systems so that steering and navigation become almost automatic.

By pre-setting waypoints in the GPS, the autohelm can be programmed to sail the boat from one point to another, altering course where required to avoid hazards or dangers, without any assistance from the navigator.

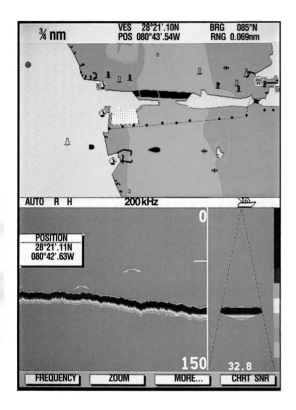

The wind vane is still widely used, and can be relied upon once it has been calibrated and adjusted to suit the individual vessel.

Modern yachts now have the option of computer-controlled steering instruments, which are far less bulky and more accurate than the mechanical gear. Autohelm electronically links a digital compass to the rudder so that the boat can be set on a predetermined course manually, or linked into an integrated electronic navigation network so the courses between waypoints are steered automatically. The latter allows for factors such as leeway or set, and incorporates automatic altering course at waypoints.

Autohelm transmits a computerized electronic signal from the compass (indicating a change in course) or the GPS (indicating that the course needs adjustment) to a motor attached to the steering gear. The motor is linked to the helm and adjusts the rudder as required. Autohelm can be fitted to either wheel or tiller steering, making it suitable for both motor and sailing boats.

The downside of automatic steering, however, is that the boat cannot detect approaching craft or unexpected dangers. Thus, although there is no need for a person to be on deck to steer the boat, it is essential that someone is on deck to keep a lookout.

Left When using a sounder and an electronic chart plotter, accuracy can be obtained for navigation in difficult areas such as harbours and shallow-water estuaries.

SOUNDERS

Modern sounders (sonar, fish finders) are a basic instrument for all forms of navigation (see page 37). They can be integrated with other electronic systems on board to form part of a network, which includes GPS, chart plotter, radar, speed log and compass. Colour or monochrome displays are available. The sounders come with a range of depths to suit either inshore fishers or the offshore ocean-crossing yacht.

They are particularly user-friendly, and the transducer can be mounted inside the hull, through the hull skin, or at the transom.

AUTOHELM

Autohelm is familiar to many sailors by its more traditional name, 'self-steering'. In essence, it is the equipment fitted to the boat so it can be steered without a person at the helm – a must for any vessel undertaking a long ocean passage or with a small crew.

Until recently, self-steering gear was mechanical and consisted of ropes and tackles or wind vanes connected to the rudder. These could be set to hold the boat on course through normal sailing conditions.

INDEX

INDEX

INDEX